"Grace—an exquisite word carrying the power of God for new covenant transformation. But that power depends on seeing all the dimensions of grace. The vulnerability of the authors, life stories of grace people, and the careful attention to theological foundation make *TrueFaced* a book to treasure. As you read with your heart and your life, you'll enter into the joy of your salvation!"

—GERRY BRESHEARS, PH.D., professor of theology, Western Seminary, Portland, Oregon

"Integrity, the consistency between inner life and outward life, is the essential character trait of a leader. The authors, by stripping away the false outward masks that hide the inner life, are stressing an essential feature of integrity. May many enter into The Room of Grace they describe."

—DR. J. ROBERT CLINTON, professor of leadership, Fuller Theological Seminary

"Masking the truth about yourself benefits no one—most significantly, you. Come clean, confess honestly, hope unswervingly, and begin living a grace-faced life! This book will help you reach that trustworthy goal."

—DR. STEPHEN A. MACCHIA, founder and president of Leadership Transformations, Inc.; author, *Becoming a Healthy Church* and *Becoming a Healthy Church Workbook*

"*TrueFaced* is a compelling invitation to pursue authenticity. This is a wonderful, liberating book full of truths that will encourage all of us to be and reveal who we really are—the people God made us to be. What a powerfully relevant message for our time!"

—DR. CRAWFORD W. LORITTS JR., author, speaker, radio host; associate director of Campus Crusade for Christ, U.S.

"*TrueFaced* helped me to continue the important journey in learning to live based on who God says I am. As I read, I was forced to lay down the book and ask myself some hard questions. It took me to places of honesty that were uncomfortable, but I emerged cleansed, ready to rest in God's love and assurance."

—BILL HULL, author, *Jesus Christ Disciple Maker,* *The Disciple-Making Pastor,* and *The Disciple-Making Church*

"While actors are at their best when they are lost in the role and are not themselves, people are at their best when they confront the illusion of the role and are themselves. By exposing the futility of masks and the power in grace, *TrueFaced* is an invitation to understand the true meaning of 'being oneself.'"

—DR. ROD K. WILSON, president, Regent College, Vancouver, Canada

"In a world where duplicity is rampant, to live with 'unveiled faces' is a great gift and is the noble dream behind *TrueFaced*."

—JOHN ORTBERG, author, *Everybody's Normal Till You Get to Know Them*

"Simple. Practical. Authentic. *TrueFaced* hits the target."

—LARRY CRABB, PH.D., author; speaker; psychologist;
founder of New Way Ministries

"This book is like a miraculous mirror—it shows us our self-imposed mask of hypocrisy and how to replace it with our true identity in Christ."

—HENRY W. HOLLOMAN, professor of systematic theology,
Talbot School of Theology, Biola University; author, *The Forgotten Blessing*

"The principles taught in *TrueFaced* will help you, as they have me, in discovering the freedom of trusting God with who you are while providing authenticity in your relationships with God and others. I will use *TrueFaced* as a guide in helping people grow in trust and spiritual maturity as they embrace God's liberating grace."

—COMMISSIONER LAWRENCE R. MORETZ, The Salvation Army, New York

"Sometimes a book can change your life. This one changed mine, and I am still learning from it. This is the best and most practical book on living by grace that I have ever read. The authors blend sound theology, deep insight, and their own stories to produce the rarest of books—one that points you straight to Christ and helps blast you into growing in your trust of him and his followers."

—DR. ROBERTA HESTENES, international minister of World Vision and
former president of Eastern University

"*TrueFaced* describes the kind of life I aspire to live—a life motivated by trusting God and others around me. If you have struggled with unresolved life issues, *TrueFaced* is the book you've been looking for. In it, you'll discover a path that leads to your healing, maturing, and releasing into the dreams God has for you."

—DR. JOSEPH M. STOWELL, president, Moody Bible Institute

"It is Christ who desires to 'unmask' me—who longs, through repentance, forgiveness, and healing, to show me my true face. Bill, Bruce, and John have listened to Jesus' heart and words regarding the 'false selves' we hide from the world behind. The way they outline is the only road to freedom from the tyranny of our hypocritical masks."

—MICHAEL CARD, musician, author, teacher

TrueFaced

TrueFaced

Trust God and Others with Who You Really Are
Experience Edition

Bill Thrall
Bruce McNicol
John Lynch

NAVPRESS

Discipleship Inside Out™

NavPress is the publishing ministry of The Navigators, an international Christian organization and leader in personal spiritual development. NavPress is committed to helping people grow spiritually and enjoy lives of meaning and hope through personal and group resources that are biblically rooted, culturally relevant, and highly practical.

For a free catalog go to www.NavPress.com

© 2004 by Bill Thrall and Bruce McNicol

ISBN 13: 978-1-57683-693-4

Cover Design: David Carlson Design
Cover Images: Digital Vision and PhotoDisc
Creative Team: Dan Rich, Liz Heaney, Arvid Wallen, Darla Hightower, Pat Reinheimer

Some of the anecdotal illustrations in this book are true to life and are included with the permission of the persons involved. All other illustrations are composites of real situations, and any resemblance to people living or dead is coincidental.

Unless otherwise identified, all Scripture quotations in this publication are taken from the HOLY BIBLE: NEW INTERNATIONAL VERSION® (NIV®). Copyright © 1973, 1978, 1984 by International Bible Society. Used by permission of Zondervan Publishing House. All rights reserved. Other versions used include: the New American Standard Bible (NASB), © The Lockman Foundation 1960, 1962, 1963, 1968, 1971, 1972, 1973, 1975, 1977; and THE MESSAGE (MSG). Copyright © 1993, 1994, 1995, 1996, 2000, 2001, 2002. Used by permission of NavPress Publishing Group.

Thrall, Bill.
  Truefaced : trust God and others with who you really are / Bill Thrall, Bruce McNicol, John Lynch.-- Rev. ed.
    p. cm.
  Includes bibliographical references.
  ISBN 1-57683-693-2
  1. Faith. 2. Trust. I. McNicol, Bruce. II. Lynch, John, 1953- III. Title.
  BV4637.T53 2004
  234'.23--dc22
                        2004007236

Printed in the United States of America

12 13 14 15 16 / 15 14 13 12 11 10

Dedication

Dedicated to all those
who keep taking the immense and sacred gamble
of trusting God and others with themselves—
enjoying the astonishing ride of living TrueFaced.

Other Books by Bill Thrall and Bruce McNicol

The Ascent of a Leader

Beyond Your Best

Contents

The Experience Edition

The message of *TrueFaced* has been making a powerful impact in many countries in its original, hardcover form. It is precisely because of that impact that we're making some changes. As we have taught this message, we have learned that there is a great need for understanding what it really means to be *TrueFaced*—and what it takes to live in an environment of grace. This is why we chose to revise *TrueFaced*.

So we began working on a *TrueFaced* Experience—a small-group experiential study—that goes beyond the pages of the book and into everyday life. As we crafted the components of this experience, we cut and revised the original book until we ended up with an affordable resource that gets to the core themes quickly—and one that is a perfect match for the rest of the experience components: the *TrueFaced Experience Guide* and the *TrueFaced Experience DVD*.

The message of *TrueFaced* remains the same: God has a ticket of destiny with your name on it—no matter how old, how broken, how tired, or how frightened you are.

If you pant for a life worth living, read on.

(For more information about the *TrueFaced Experience Guide* and *TrueFaced Experience DVD*, visit www.navpress.com or call 1-800-366-7788

CHAPTER ONE

Keeping Up Appearances

Away and mock the time with fairest show;
False face must hide what the false heart doth know.
—Shakespeare, *Macbeth*

Ever since we were children we have had dreams and hopes of destiny. Some of these dreams are our own, but others came from the very heart of God—and God's dreams never go off the radar screen. Even time, failure, or heartbreak can't make us forget them entirely. Still, most of us have tried to stuff them into the attic. We have been rudely awakened out of too many of them, too many times, and each time we lost more and more of the dream. Yet, even if we've forgotten the fiber of those dreams, God has not.

God dreams that you would discover your destiny and walk into the reasons he placed you on this earth. God has a ticket of destiny with your name written on it—no matter how old, how broken, how tired, or how frightened you are. No matter how many times you may have failed, God dearly longs for the day when he gets to hand you that ticket, smile, and whisper into your ear, "You have no idea how long I've waited to hand this to you. Have a blast! I've already seen what you get to do. It's better than you could have dreamed. Now hurry up and get on that train. A whole lot of folk are waiting for you to walk into your destiny and into their lives."

Wow! How stunningly incredible! Yet many of us read these words of hope and think, *Can you possibly have any idea how much I want to believe that? But if this is true, if these words are really true, then someone tell me—what has happened to my life! I have had those dreams. I've experienced them in the core of my soul. I believe God has such dreams for me. But every attempt to step into these dreams has been a repeated scene of shooting myself in the foot. The circumstances change, but the shooting and my foot are in each scene. After each repeated failure, I have less confidence anything will ever change. I have these longings, these dreams, that I've always thought were from God, aching to be released. But far more often I just hurt, confuse, and frustrate the very people and environments I long to bless. It's as if nobody but me can see the dream, and there are insurmountable obstacles at every turn. And though I blame others, I'm pretty sure most of the obstacles have to do with me. I'm not even sure what I'm doing wrong to thwart each effort. I just do. I'm so preoccupied with my own issues that I can't even make sense of this moment, let alone the dream. It feels like I will never be fit, prepared, or matured to match the beauty and grandeur of what I've seen in the distance. The dreams are becoming cruel mirages, shimmering pools of once naive hope, now melted. I fear I am becoming jaded to such dreaming and am settling into a gray existence of sleepy living in a land where it is always desert with no oasis.*

So, here's the not-so-small print that maybe you never read at the start of your journey: God's dreams for you are ultimately not really about *you*. Oh, don't misunderstand. They'll bring you some of the best days of your life; you will be fulfilled beyond any imaginable expectations. But God's dreams take form only when they are about others, for the benefit of others. Loving them. Guiding them. Serving them. Influencing them. Filling their heads with dreams and hope. There are no other types of God dreams. Nothing less or else will compel, attract, or seem worthy of this God heart within you. Everything else will always, ultimately, taste chalky and dry. God's destiny for you will never be so trivial as building a kingdom for you to enhance your acclaim. Such is a kingdom of dust and lint. The dream he has prepared custom for you is explosively beautiful and alive. It's about his glorious kingdom—a plan involving you from before there was time! This stunning dream always involves others. Others being freed, healed, convinced of who they really are, convinced that they can fly, convinced his dreams in them can come true. This unbending intention of God has been at once the source of your best dreaming and your continuous foot shooting.

Think about it—God's dreams for us reflect *his* heart. If we are not maturing in sync with his heart, how would we distinguish *others-centered* dreams from *self-centered* dreams? Many of us remain so wounded and preoccupied with our own stuff that we concoct our own tepid, cheap dreams and call them God's. After a while we wouldn't recognize God's dream for us if it came up and shouted, "Howdy, I'm your dream!"

God wants to reveal himself to us in authenticity. Because one of God's dreams is that we would influence others far more out of *who* we are than out of what we do. So, above all else, your destiny requires that you be a maturing person. The Father wants us to mature into the "likeness of his Son," because he can't release us into his dreams for us unless we are maturing.

We wrote *TrueFaced* for those who pant for a life worth living. We wrote *TrueFaced* for those who have tasted of their destiny, but have lost its flavor in brokenhearted disappointment. We wrote *TrueFaced* for those suffocating under hope-stifling masks. We wrote *TrueFaced* for those longing to see their God with eyes no longer filtered with fear, self-disgust, and desperate proving.

Remember the first time you came face-to-face with the self-sufficient life and came to despise it? Remember humbly admitting to God who you really were? Right about then you met Jesus—and experienced this kind of hope in a way you had never before imagined.

God couldn't help us until we trusted him with who we really were. That was perhaps our first taste of a *TrueFaced* life. It was stunning. Incredible. It painted our world in colors we hardly knew existed. But, something happened to many of us in the intervening years. We lost confidence that his delight *of* us and new life *in* us would be a strong enough impetus for a growth that would glorify God and fix our junk. So, we gradually bought the slick sales pitch that told us we would need to find something more, something others seemed to have that we could never quite get our hands around. Something magical and mystical that we would receive if we tried hard enough and proved good enough, often enough. And so we began learning to prop things up. We went back to trying to impress God and others—back to posturing, positioning, manipulating, trying to appear better than who we were. Our two-faced life has severely stunted our growth. And broken our hearts. And left us gasping. Although we may have accumulated titles, status, and accomplishments, we personally remain wounded and immature—long on "success," but short on dreams. We admire people who live the *TrueFaced* life, but our loss of hope has forced us into desperately trying to discover safety from behind our masks. In a very real sense, we are *all* performers. Because of sin we've lost confidence that we will always please our audience, and so we put on a mask. As an unintended result, no one, not even the people we love, ever get to see our true face.

John fashioned an elaborate mask shortly after he graduated from Arizona State University in 1975. He hadn't given much thought about his future; he had just assumed it would come knocking at his door.

As May neared, his classmates started telling him about their soon-to-be-launched careers in companies such as IBM, Xerox, and Fidelity Mutual. His friends had secured real, actual careers—complete with salaries and benefits! After bragging about their bright futures, his classmates would inevitably ask, "So, how about you, John? What field are you going into?"

"Well . . . I'm . . . uh . . . keeping my options open. I've got a lot of brands in the fire. I don't want to bite at the first thing to come along."

In truth, John had nothing in the fire, but admitting that felt way too risky. So he made two significant decisions. First, without telling anyone, he moved to Isla Vista, a small beach town near Santa Barbara, California—a town where no one knew him and where those who did couldn't find him.

Second, he wrote to everyone he knew, and told them, "Hey, I found a gig in Isla Vista. I can't believe it! I'm the featured weekend comedy act at a nightclub named Borsody's. I've worked up a bunch of new bits, local kinds of stuff. Just a couple of Saturdays ago a talent guy asked the manager if he could use me a couple nights in L.A.! Well, stay in touch. I'll write more later. I've gotta work on tonight's show."

Actually, Isla Vista did have a nightclub named Borsody's. John just made up a few of the surrounding details.

With that letter, John fashioned a mask that he thought would protect him from his friends' pity. The trouble is, once we put on a mask, we have a hard time taking it off. John kept that particular mask on for four and a half years! It had become his identity.

After a while the mask began to deceive even him. The lie rolled off of his tongue so easily that he began to believe it was part of his history—that he actually had been a comedian at Borsody's! When he describes that time in his life, John says, "I could see the smoke-filled room and the hurricane lamps at each table. I could see the light spilling onto a stage with a stool and a mike that sent my voice out into a dark sea of smiling faces. I could hear the audience's laughter and smell the beer. Now that's a mask!"

Unknown to him, John's mask was actually as thin as sketch paper. People could see right through it. Years later, he asked a few of his friends, "Did you believe me? Did you wonder if I actually was doing stand-up comedy?"

One of his best friends told him, "We never talked much about it. We just loved you. We figured that if it weren't true, it probably wouldn't help for us to blow your cover. No, I guess I never really thought you were doing stand-up."

Wow! John had told himself that he had on wonderful, hip clothes: "I thought my friends were proud of me. I thought they believed I was somebody significant and famous. What a waste of energy and soul. The papier-mâché mask I thought would protect me by covering up the truth didn't. In fact, it had the opposite effect—it caused me to be the object of my friends' pity. If only I had just waited tables."

Some of us reading this might be thinking, *Whew! I'm glad I'm not like John. Imagine, lying to people about who you are! Making up stories and almost believing them yourself! That's messed up!*

It's true. Pretending to be someone you are not *is* messed up . . . messed up like the president of the United States Olympic Committee Sandy Baldwin, who suddenly lost her position for lying on her résumé about her education. Or messed up like Philippine President Joseph Ejercito Estrada, who banked on macho charisma and pro-poor platforms while breaking the law "like clockwork." Estrada held millions in illicit funds through a network of hidden bank accounts. Or messed up like Alabama District Judge Jack Montgomery, who, under cover of the justice system, extorted bribes from defendants. Or like Tom Collen, whose résumé "errors" cost him his new job as Vanderbilt's women's basketball coach. Or like Martin Frankel, the financier who took control of seven U.S. insurance companies and embezzled more than two hundred million dollars before fleeing to Rome in a private jet. Or messed up like, um, well, like King Saul when he said, "I did obey God."[1]

Adam and Eve's Legacy

Do you remember how mask-wearing got started? God comes in the cool of the day to be with Adam and Eve after the "apple incident." He calls out to a hiding Adam, "Where are you?"—knowing very well where Adam is. Adam responds, "I heard the sound of *You* in the garden, and I was *afraid* because I was naked; so I *hid* myself."[2]

There they are, the opening steps to the dance of mask-wearing— I become afraid because something I did or was done to me made me feel naked. And this nakedness cried out to be covered. Nothing feels more frightening or lonely than nakedness. And not knowing how to allow myself to be covered, I hid myself. Every dance of mask-wearing follows such steps. This shame, this self-perception of embarrassment and being "dirty," prompted Adam and Eve to fashion masks from leaves in order to hide what was true about them.[3]

That day all humanity learned how to look over our shoulders, how to glance furtively, how to say one thing and mean another, how to hide fear, deceit, and shame behind a thin smile. That day we learned how to give the appearance we are someone other than who we actually are. And we've developed it into an art form! (Thanks, Adam and Eve. Nice legacy.) But gradually, we lose all hope that we can change or be "fixed." So we cover up. We put on a mask and begin bluffing. Mask wearers usually fall into one of three groups: those living in the Land of "Doing Just Fine," those searching for the next "new" technique, or those wearing pedigreed masks.

The Land of "Doing Just Fine"

Those of us who live in the Land of "Doing Just Fine" are surrounded by nicely scrubbed folk who smile broadly and shake each others' hand firmly. Our conversations go something like this:

"Hi, Milo. How ya doin'?"

"Doin' fine, Mitch. Yourself?"

"Fine, Milo. Fine. Couldn't be finer. Fine day, eh?"

"Fine indeed, Milo. Oh, hi, Mildred. How ya doin'?"

"Well, hello, Mitch. I'm doin' fine, considering the circumstances. Just fine. Fine day we're having."

"Yes, it is Mildred. Fine as fine can be. How's that husband of yours?"

"Well, Mitch, he's doin' fine too. Whole family's doin' just fine. Can't complain. Yep, I just spoke to Mrs. Sanderson and she told me that she was doing fine, but she had it on reliable information that several other unnamed families were *not* doing fine. She asked that I not share that publicly, but I tell you, only so you might pray more effectively."

"Well, that's fine with me, Mildred. At least we're fine . . . just fine."

The time has come for those of us who say we are "doin' just fine" to acknowledge the truth: We are not fine, not fine at all. We're hurting. We're lonely, confused, and frightened. We are convinced there is no real help for our issues and that the best thing we can do is to hide our true identities. It's time to admit what we're really thinking: *You have no idea who I am. Nobody knows who I am. Nobody. Not even my spouse. I'm surrounded by friends and family, but they don't know me. Every time I enter a room, it's with a persona as big as I am. I posture and position and pontificate. I can make small talk. I can even enter into meaningful, deep, theological discussion. But the person you see is made up on the run, while the real me frantically operates the levers from behind a mask. I leave almost every encounter desperately alone and feeling deeply unknown.*

If we could take off our masks, many in this group would say, "I'm tired . . . *really* tired. I'm weary of hurting and weary of dragging myself one more time through the same hoops I've tried hundreds of times before. I feel betrayed—betrayed by what I have been taught, betrayed by my own behavior, and betrayed by my community of faith. Everyone there seems to be 'doing just fine.' Yet few seem to be living the answers they've been giving.[4] And most of all, I feel betrayed by God himself."

Still Searching for the Next "New" Technique

Those of us who make up this next group go from book to book, seminar to seminar, church to church looking for the next new technique promising to help change us. We've admitted that life isn't "just fine." Our frustration permeates our thoughts: *Life isn't working for me. I've tried to honor the life I thought I was supposed to live, but it's not paying off like I thought it would. Give me something I can jam into my current game plan that will fix me without too much pain and change.*

But like dieters on their eleventh "new plan," those in this group grow increasingly more disillusioned and skeptical. We've been putting bailing wire on the issues of our lives. And we know it. There *must* be an answer. There *has* to be. The God we've trusted would never just play with our heads . . . would he? We have convinced ourselves that there are answers, but we're befuddled that we can't find them.

This twisted line of reasoning begins to creep into our thinking: *What's wrong with me? Nothing I try works. Maybe, after what I've done, I don't deserve answers. After all, others seem to figure out this stuff, but I am not changing. Nothing seems to be getting me to the abundant life that I'm supposed to be experiencing.*

We read about concepts and strategies that have promised to change us, but we remain ultimately unchanged . . . and we know it . . . and we fear that others are beginning to know it. Oh, we've learned a new vocabulary and can rearrange the lawn furniture of our behaviors, but deep inside, we know we're little different than we were. We believe that if others could spend a moment inside us they would be disgusted by what they discover. We're appalled because we have already discovered it. And we are deeply afraid that they will discover the truth about us. So we pretend to be someone we are not. And this hidden, pretend person disgusts us most.

We're starting to lose all hope that we can change. We suspect that what we are missing is hidden from our understanding or ability to fix. We feel stuck in our deep insecurity and shame. So, we continue to bluff. We marshal all of our best appearances and smile a lot.

At this point, some of us are likely thinking, *What's wrong with these people? Why can't they get their act together?* If so, we are part of the third group.

The Pedigreed Mask

We are the "together" folk, the postcard family: well-educated, well-heeled, well-groomed, well-assured . . . and, well, a lot of work for the rest of us.

Quite frankly, our life doesn't really have this messy stuff in it. It all just slides right off. Our home and family and hobbies are almost as perfect as we are. We don't need help or answers; we are help and answers. Always well stocked with teaching for others, we have little need of anyone to teach us. It is all working for us. We are the standard by which the industry is judged. We are right, and if only others could learn from us, they would be able to get on with their little lives. Our behavior is airtight and we know we are morally superior. We are not vulnerable. We don't need to be, for we are self-sufficient.[5]

We intimidate others, but we know it's because they are jealous. If they had our self-determination and discipline they wouldn't have to be intimidated. If they have an issue with us, well, then it's all about them. Our goal is to get around them, get rid of them, or get over them.

This book may be for those of us in this group most of all, for we are in desperate need. We deny that we even wear a mask, but the truth about us is this: Those who know us best wish they could tell us that, while our résumé is impressive, our mask is coming apart. They long to get past our mask so that they could love us and know us and know our love, but we have kept them at such a distance that they have given up. We are truly emperors wearing no clothes.

What's Behind the Choice to Wear a Mask?

Most of us will readily admit, "I know I wear masks. Sometimes I feel like I'm working off a prepared script. I'll say the most trite-sounding things in order to cover my real feelings. I don't really like this about me, but I have no idea how to take my masks off. If I did, I don't think I would be in this mess."

We're in the dark about how we got like this. We blame our actions on circumstances or the pressure we're under. "I must be going through menopause or a midlife crisis," we say. And that makes sense, until we are reminded that we aren't yet forty!

One of the really good gifts we could receive would be the ability to see where we are and how we got here. We need to see ourselves in our story, to see what causes and drives the responses that trip us up. We must see that our controlling behavior isn't a response to something happening in the present. It is triggered by some sin in the past that never got resolved. If we can begin to understand the process of unresolved sin and discover what is happening to us, we may no longer react to life like lemmings heading for the nearest cliff. You see, mask-wearing, though a horrible problem, is not the underlying problem. It is the pitiful symptom of the larger problem: unresolved sin issues. A mask is only the public proof that an infection is spreading through my body. Inside me, there is a seditious, self-destructive process compelling me to hide what is really true about me. It is time to unmask this dark dynamic that compels me to fashion a mask.

Our Real Problem

When we sin or when someone else sins against us, we experience some automatic responses. If we do the sinning, our automatic response is called *guilt*.[6] If someone else sins against us, our automatic response is called *hurt*.[7] God designed these two responses to tell us that something wrong has happened, that something just got fractured and needs healing. We don't have to work at producing these two responses to sin. Guilt and hurt are involuntary. Instinctive.

Most of us don't know what to do with these internal responses to sin. Like Adam, we feel naked, so we try to hide or override our guilt or hurt. At the moment, it seems like self-preservation. But that choice makes our life confusing, twisted, and dark in a hurry and unleashes a new depth of pain, inner turmoil, and mask-wearing.

Like an undiagnosed disease quietly spreading poison throughout our bloodstream, the decision to hide or ignore our guilt and hurt leaves the *act of sin* unresolved. We may recognize we don't have the energy we used to have, but we blame this on something or someone else and fail to recognize and understand that an invisible, inner enemy drains our energy and joy. We may try to ignore it or stuff it away, but though it may lie dormant for a while, unresolved sin is always buried *alive*.

It's as if we've wrenched our back, wrenched it for the fourth time over the last three months. We try to convince ourselves that the problem can be solved with a bag of ice cubes. After a couple of days, the pain subsides. Other than occasional stiffness, we basically just forget about it. We figure we've dodged the bullet of the chiropractor. Then one day we drop our keys in the Wal-Mart parking lot. As we bend down to pick them up, we suddenly fall to our knees with a yelp. Hunched over, we look to passersby like a deeply devout person suddenly moved to pray. Several high-school kids see us and help us back into our car. One of them cautions the others to be careful because "older people's bones are more brittle." Suddenly, the tiniest wrong move has made us walk like one of the early figures on an evolutionary wall chart. We require two days of bed rest, watching infomercials about basting ovens.

We have "Wal-Mart parking lot experiences" precisely because nothing in us can absorb sin. Nothing. *Even* when we are the one being sinned against, we still cannot handle sin, because sin done to us will *always ignite the nature of the sin already in us*. So, we give ourselves permission to act out sinfully. Twisted, isn't it? It all makes us want to scream, "That isn't fair. I wasn't the one who started this. I wasn't the one who sinned!" And we're right. It is not fair. Sin does not play fair.[8]

The good news is that we can stop the damage at any time by applying God's resources and power to resolve that sin. But if we don't access God's resources, the devastating pattern continues — our guilt or hurt will then morph into half a dozen or more ugly responses, which we call Inevitable Effects: shame, blame, fear, denial, anger, and their assorted sickly relatives. Something under our own roof begins to destroy us! How sad is that? Most of us are clueless about this chain reaction. We only know we have deep, painful feelings; distorted, dysfunctional thoughts; and befuddling behaviors that we feel an almost involuntary need to mask.

Six of the many damaging behaviors resulting from unresolved sin:

1. I become highly sensitized to my own sin and judge the sin of others.
2. I lose my objectivity in a crisis and I become the issue.
3. I hide my sinful behavior and become vulnerable to more sin.
4. I am unable to be loved or to love.
5. I become susceptible to wrong life choices.
6. I attempt to control others.

But our futile disguise simply tells others that we have problems. They don't know why we're acting so oddly. They just pity us. Or talk about us. Or find socially acceptable ways to keep their distance. We're not unlike a tourist trying to impress his waiter by bluffing fluency in another language, oblivious that instead of medallions of lamb he just ordered a dish of metal fasteners. He unwittingly becomes the subject of much ridicule and mockery back in the kitchen.

Sharon's Story

To help explain just how destructive this process of unresolved sin can be, we've asked a good friend of ours, Sharon, to tell her story. It's the story of how acts of sin against her, which remained unresolved for years, played themselves out in her life.

Sharon grew up in a family well respected as great teachers, worship leaders, and community pillars. As a young girl, she was poised, attractive, intelligent, and charming. She had enormous potential, drive, and passion. But as a young adult, she would, now and then, unexpectedly erupt in rage over something fairly insignificant. For the most part, her friends chalked it up to the eccentricities of an unusually gifted person.

As Sharon became an adult, her responsibilities began to match her growing proficiency. But she didn't smile as much. She found herself lashing out at her new husband. To those close to her, she was an enigma. She could demonstrate tremendous kindness and goodness, and yet more and more often she was given to fits of rage, judgment, criticism, and blame. With a growing air of superiority, she entered her thirties. She became incredibly driven and spent more and more time alone.

How did this happen? What could cause these increasing displays of pain in a seemingly together person? We'll let Sharon tell you herself:

> What I heard in church and what I experienced at home were two very different things. My "Christian" parents sinned violently against me. My father and many other men used me sexually, and my mother knew of it. Whenever I resisted, my parents would twist Scripture by saying that children are to obey their parents "in all things."
>
> My parents did further harm to me by repeatedly telling me I was born with the "wrong personality." I knew that God had created me to be a leader, but my parents manipulated Scripture to demean the place of women in God's eyes. Their abuse and legalism wounded me deeply.
>
> As a child I wasn't able to bring to God the *acts of sin* done against me. I couldn't even understand what was happening to me, and because I did not know how to resolve my hurt, a torrent of *Inevitable Effects* was unleashed in my life.
>
> The sexual abuse left me with physical scars. I also

had emotional scars from years of neglect and deep spiritual wounds from my confusion between what I read in the Bible and what I had experienced. I grew up believing I was unlovable. I was only worthy to be used and hated, never to be protected. Now I was desperately trying to be the "right" kind of woman. But I didn't even understand who I was. But the deepest wound was my heart's lack of hope that anyone could ever love me.

I became very skilled at hiding my shame—or so I hoped. I learned to change my behavior to fit whatever spiritual culture I was in. I became very judgmental of others in an attempt to feel better about myself. I buried my hurt under an intense rage. Anger was my means to being in control. I had become proficient at blaming.

My self-protective behaviors kept me from getting my real needs met. *The sin done to me inflamed my own sin—and I didn't know what to do about it.* I didn't trust anyone. I felt alone, unsafe, and unlovable, long after I was far from my parents' home.

Out of God's abundant grace, I got married and had two children. But I could not continually wear my mask of the perfect, godly woman. I unleashed my anger at home, on my husband and kids. I was hypocritical. I didn't want to continue pretending to be someone I wasn't.

I was finally around people who wanted me to be the person I was created to be, but I had absolutely no idea how to let myself be it! My masks that once felt protective were now suffocating me! The hurt, buried under my anger, was trying to surface and I didn't know how to go to God with it. I was bitter at my parents and my siblings. I was resentful of my husband for not meeting my needs. I was a toxic person to those closest to me. I was everything I didn't want to be, and it caused me to feel even more unlovable. And I couldn't stop it.

We'll return to Sharon's story in chapter 4. But don't miss this truth: Whenever we are unable or unwilling to deal with the guilt or hurt of sin done by us or to us, something very much like Sharon's erratic and destructive response overruns *our* landscape. Then pain and confusion floods our lives and those around us.

But How Can I Know If I Have Unresolved Sin?

When an act of sin remains unresolved, it causes *a nagging sense in the heart that doesn't go away*. Note that it's a "nagging" sense. We're in no way describing a morbid search to uncover some deep, hidden sin, or, as one friend calls it, "that elusive omission I think is keeping me from God's will." No, unresolved junk will remind us of itself on a regular basis. We'll never have to search for it. But like plaque, cholesterol, or unanswered e-mail, unresolved sin builds up. Eventually we have so much junk in our lives that we're convinced God can barely tolerate us. There's a dried out kettle of spoiled herring for you!

This process of unresolved sin plays out in every person, including those who don't follow Christ. The only real difference between them and Christ followers is the hope of a solution. But when we refuse, deny, or misplace God's provision for that hope, we lay ourselves open to an endless variety of counterfeits peddling a promise of relief: We start trusting techniques, conscience-numbing medication, pop psychology, spiritual fads, and a hundred other nicely packaged weasels. Whenever we sin and don't resolve that sin, either because we don't know how or choose not to, we release an inevitable force that drains our confidence in who we really are.

Next thing we know, we're looking for a top-of-the-line mask, maybe several. We hastily snatch them up from dozens of designer options: "I'm better than most," "I'm very together," "I don't really care," "I am self-sufficient," "I'm very important," "I'm competent enough to be loved," "I am competent enough not to need love," "I have the answers," "I'm independent," or "I am cool." But all the while, our heart whispers: "You're a fake, an impostor, a loser. You always have been. You always will be. You may fool others, but I know who you are. You're a joke, the definition of hypocrite. You have no self-respect. You spent it long ago."

The High Cost of a Two-Faced Life

It is very expensive to wear a mask. For one thing, no one—not even those I love—ever gets to see my face. There are moments when some hint of the real me bleeds through, but mostly I just confuse them. Worse yet, I never experience the love of others because when I wear a mask, only my mask receives love! I sense I'm still not loved and self-diagnose that maybe my mask wasn't good or tight enough. So, I delve even more desperately into mask-wearing, convinced maybe the next one will present what you want and prove I'm worthy to receive your love. And if that's not painful enough, get this. I also cannot give love from behind a mask, at least not love from the real me. The ones I long to love experience the cloying attempts of someone who doesn't exist.

Many of us just stopped on those last few sentences and sighed at the realization of wasted love and unnecessary loneliness. But even all of that is not all of that. Mask-wearing thwarts our maturing, the very path into the dreams God intended for us. God designed release of influence this way on purpose, because immature people have an incredibly negative impact on those they influence. When we don a mask, we convince others that:

- They too must live a two-faced life.
- They too must present an idealized person.
- They too must hide what is true about them.
- New life in Christ doesn't really work.
- They will remain stuck in their unresolved life issues.
- It is better to be unknown than to risk rejection.
- Self-protection is their only hope.

When we wear masks, we teach others:

- To live in guarded fear.
- To live a life of comparison, envy, and jealousy.
- To trade vulnerability for the veneer of safety.

So, we're not just actors. We are also directors in a badly styled play, teaching those we love how to pose and masquerade, memorize fake lines, rehearse expressions, and produce false tears on command.

Sadly, cruelly, our masks deceive us into believing that we can hide our true selves. Not so. In time, others can usually see what we're trying to hide. No matter how beautifully formed, our masks eventually present us as tragic figures . . . because masks always crack or distort or buckle or unravel or wear through or lose their shape.

Christ Followers in Denial

Perhaps you are thinking, *This can't be me they're talking about. The mask came off when I became a Christian and I have no reason to put on another one! I mean, John couldn't have been a Christ-follower in college. No wonder he masked his life.*

You're right; John was not a Christian in college — in spades. At age twenty-seven, John's high-school students led him to know and trust Jesus. And wouldn't you know, from that time on, John never picked up a mask again . . . at least not for several weeks. The truth is, since the day he came to Christ, John has put on more masks than an actor in a traveling Kabuki theater group! Every time he retreats from trusting Jesus, a Pandora's box opens, and John is tempted again to put on a mask. Why? Because he's frightened at what he sees inside himself.[9] He doesn't want to reveal his true face.

If this shocks us, it shouldn't . . . not if we are being honest.

A large percentage of us have done something similar. Many of us are hurting. We harbor painful junk that is eating us alive. And we live in a "family" sending this unspoken message: "I prefer that you be who I want you to be rather than who you are, if it's all the same to you." So when things break down in our gig, the mask goes on and the charade begins — and everyone, *everyone*, loses.

People wear masks for all sorts of reasons. Some of us opt for a mask because we fear we might not be accepted or, worse, that we may be viewed as unworthy of acceptance because we have *already* proven ourselves unacceptable. Perhaps we wear a mask because we fear that others won't protect us and might leave us feeling naked and alone. Or we fear that others *will* protect us, but our protection will come at the price of their control.

Bruce feels threatened when a person in a key relationship doubts his motives or trustworthiness. He instinctively withdraws from that person by putting on an "I don't really care" mask. Bill dons an "I'm not hurt" mask when he feels insecure and fears being abandoned. John puts on the "I am self-sufficient" mask any time he fears someone's pity.

You see, mask-wearing is often even more pronounced in Christians. Youch! All mask-wearing is a product of pretending something to be true in our lives that our experience denies. Our pretending may be fueled by a sincere desire to make God look good by having our act together. He has no need for such help, but we think it is our duty, nonetheless. So, we cover our dirty laundry and think we're doing the right thing by "modeling" to the world how well God improves the lives of Christians. Instead, we usually just come off as weird, stiffly religious, proud, and working way too hard.

All of us need to be able to recognize our patterns of hiding. We need to understand how wearing a mask has affected our relationships, stopped our maturing, and thwarted our dreams. Do not jam this fresh look at timeless truth into old boxes. Please don't presume you already get this stuff, or read with somebody else in mind, or you might just blissfully skip through this book and miss God's call to your heart.

The Wonderful News

We named this book *TrueFaced* for several reasons. First, we wanted to communicate that almost all of us, at some time, resort to appearances, to mask-wearing. You are not some freak of nature if you see yourself in these chapters. Second, we wanted to point out that eventually our masks always begin to crack.

This is wonderful news.

"What?" you ask with high-pitched incredulity. "I've worked all my adult life to keep my mask from cracking. How could that possibly be anything but the worst news?"

Well, imagine if the mask didn't crack. If our masks succeeded in their attempts at self-protection, thus keeping us from love, trust, authenticity, and freedom, then we might go our entire lives missing out on what we were created for. So God allows our masks to crack and chip and distort because he loves us so much.

Which brings us to the third reason for the book's title. In this book we present truths that can help you begin, by God's grace, to reveal your true face. It's a really cool face. God made it and can't wait to see his reflection in it.[10] Those who love you can't wait to see it either. It's the *TrueFaced* life that leads to the maturing and dreams for which we all long. As a friend has said when describing her life behind the mask, "The trouble with papier-mâché is that it doesn't reflect."

How we wish that all of us—those who know Jesus and those simply curious about him—could give ourselves permission to ask throughout this book, "Could this be *me* they're describing? What if these things were actually true about *me*?"

After the Mask Cracks

Maybe you are beginning to suspect your mask has a crack. Maybe you are ready to ask some hard questions. Welcome aboard, friend. It is a journey many of us are walking.

When we admit that the old answers don't work anymore, we stop reading authors with nice-sounding platitudes and slogans, and we become hungry for books that don't deny pain or tell you to keep trying what hasn't worked before. Alongside others in a fragile community of grace, the three of us who wrote this book are learning these truths. We are on the same journey; hungry for the promises of this life Jesus offered and still offers.

Call out to the living God, "Father, is this me they're describing? Can you show me a way out of this maze? It's all I've ever known. I know you long for it to be different between you and me. I know you long for my life to count and for me to experience joy, hope, and the dreams you have for me. I have nothing to lose but a life that wasn't working anyway. Come reveal to me my true face, reflecting yours."

⎓ DID YOU DISCOVER?

- We've lost our confidence that we will always please our audience, so we feel compelled to hide and put on a mask.

- There are dozens of masks in the wardrobe from which to choose.

- An unresolved sin is a known sin that creates a nagging sense in the heart that doesn't go away.

- Hope begins by understanding this critical point: both the one who sins and the one sinned against have an *involuntary response* of the heart to an *act of sin*.

  - In the one who sins, the effect is guilt.

  - In the one who is sinned against, the effect is hurt.

- The decision to ignore our sin creates *unresolved sin*, which is like an undiagnosed disease that quietly spreads poison throughout our bloodstream.

- Most of us fall into one of three groups: those who pretend things are just fine, those searching for new techniques to get better, and those who wear "pedigreed masks."

- Mask-wearing is sometimes even more pronounced in Christians than in those still seeking Christ.

- God wants to see his reflection in our faces, but the trouble with papier-mâché is that it doesn't reflect.

- This book is named *TrueFaced* because we all resort to appearances and struggle to find our true faces, and second, because a wonderful opportunity for healing and maturing eventually occurs—our masks begin to crack.

CHAPTER TWO

To Please or to Trust?

Two roads diverged in a wood, and I,
I took the one less traveled by, and that has made all the difference.
—Robert Frost

≡ . . . **A**nd so the day comes when we are forced to choose. Eventually, we each find ourselves arriving at a pivotal place on our journey with God. We stand before two roads diverging in the woods, and our choice will make all the difference. We may not even realize we are making this choice, but we all make it many times on our journey. It's the most important ongoing decision any of us will make as Christians.

As we're walking down life's road, we arrive at a tall pole with signs pointing in two different directions. The marker leading to the left simply says Pleasing God. The one leading to the right reads Trusting God. It's hard to choose one over the other, because both roads have a good feel to them. We discover there is no third road and it becomes obvious that we will not be able to jump back and forth between the paths. We must choose one. *Only* one. It will now indelibly mark the way we live.

Pleasing God and Trusting God represent the primary and ultimate motives of our hearts, the inner drives or desires that cause us to act in a certain way. These motives, in turn, produce multiple actions:

Motive → Values → Actions

Pleasing God and Trusting God are both admirable, but since I can have only one primary motive, I ask myself, "Which of these motives best reflects the relationship I want to have with God?"

In the end, I choose the path marked Pleasing God. The Trusting God path just seems too, well, passive. I want a fully alive experience with God. The Pleasing God path seems like the best way there. I think, *All right then, my mind's made up. I am determined to please God. I so long for him to be happy with me. I'll discipline myself to achieve this life goal. I know I can do it. Yes, I will do it this time. I will please him and he will be pleased with me.* So we set off with confidence. We are immediately comforted to see that the path is well traveled.

In time I come to a door with a sign that reads Striving to Be All God Wants Me to Be. These words reflect the values that flow out of the motive of Pleasing God, and they describe how we believe we should act. Since my motive is a determination to please God, I will value being all God wants me to be. So, I open the door by turning the knob of Effort. The motive of Pleasing God has now produced the value of Striving to Be All God Wants Me to Be. As I enter this enormous room, a hostess with a beautiful smile greets me and says in an almost too polite tone, "Welcome to The Room of Good Intentions."

Oh, yes. I like the ring of this name. I also like being perceived as someone who is well intended. "Well, thanks," I answer. "I think I've found my home. How are you?"

The hostess pauses for a moment and then reaches into her purse to pull out a mask bearing a guarded expression and a thin smile. She puts it on and answers, "Fine. Just fine. And you?"

The entire room gets suddenly quiet, awaiting my answer. "Well, umm, thanks for asking. I'm kind of struggling with some things right now, some areas that don't seem to be in keeping with who I know I'm supposed to be. I'm not really sure I'm doing well on a lot of—" The hostess cuts me off, putting her finger to her lips and handing me a similar mask. I'm not quite sure what to do. I don't really want to put it on, but others in the room are smiling and motioning for me to do so. I want so much to be accepted here that I slowly put it on.

And now everything feels different. I am quickly overcome with the realization that less self-revelation would be a smart game plan here. I realize that no one in this room wants to hear about my struggles, pain, or doubt. If I want to be welcome here, I'd better keep my cards closer to my vest and give the appearance of sufficiency. So, I slowly and carefully say the words, "Actually, I'm fine. I'm doing just fine. Thanks." Satisfied, everyone in the room turns back to their conversations.

You see, everyone in The Room of Good Intentions has the value of Striving to Be All God Wants Them to Be. They are sincerely determined to be godly. Their value produces actions that are best summarized by an enormous banner on the back wall that reads, Working on My Sin to Achieve an Intimate Relationship with God. They have made it their goal to be godly, and they fully expect the same of everyone else in the room.

As I read the words on the banner, I can't help but think, *Sounds a lot like, "Be holy as your heavenly Father is holy."*[1] *Yep. I'm in the right place. The people here have sincerity, perseverance, courage, diligence, full-hearted fervency, a desire to please God, and a sold-out determination to pursue excellence. Yes, this is the place I've been looking for. Oh, I'm going to make him so happy. One day soon, we will be close. I just know it!*

Yet, as weeks turn into months, I can't help noticing that many people in this room sound a bit cynical and look pretty tired. Many of them seem alone. And if I catch them when they think no one is looking, I see incredible pain on their faces. Quite a few seem superficial—guarded. After a while I realize that my thinking has begun shifting too. I no longer feel as comfortable or relaxed here. I have this nagging anxiety that if I don't keep behaving well—if I don't control my sin enough—I'll be on the outs with everyone in the room. And with God!

So, I start investing more effort into sinning less, and I feel better . . . for a while. But the more time I spend in The Room of Good Intentions, the more disappointment I feel. Despite all my striving, all my efforts, I keep sinning! In fact, some days I'm fixated simply on trying *not* to sin. I seem to never be able to get around to doing things to please God. It takes all my energy to avoid doing those things that *displease* him! Other days I can't seem to do enough. I never get through my list of things to work on. It feels like I am making every effort to please a God who never seems pleased enough! I carry an overwhelming sense of guilt because I have to hide my sin—from everyone in the room and from God. Gradually, almost imperceptibly, the road of Pleasing God has turned into What Must I Do to Keep God Pleased with Me?

The stifling atmosphere in the room and the tightness of my mask make it hard for me to breathe. I am so tired of pretending and keeping up appearances.

As I search for the door, someone walks up to me and, looking over his shoulder, whispers, "Hey, umm, I'm going to check out that other path back at the crossroads. For the last several years, I've given this room everything I've got, and something's not working for me. You look tired too. You want to go retrace our steps and head out for the Trusting God trail?"

I Took the Road Less Traveled . . .

So back I go to the fork in the road. Hmmm. It still feels wrong to take the road marked Trusting God—as if I'd be getting away with something. I look around for a third road, maybe some combination of the two, but no such luck. There are just the two roads. Still. The road of Trusting God sure sounds a lot less heroic than the other. A bit ethereal and vague. And it appears to give me nothing much to do other than, well . . . trust. All I ever heard in the Room of Good Intentions was that I have to "sell out, care more, get on fire, buck up, shape up, and tighten up." This road doesn't seem to give me any of that. But I think, *I'm only risking a little time and effort. I can always head back to the Pleasing God path if this turns out to be a dead end. Besides the cracks in my mask are getting bigger and bigger—I don't know how long I can keep bluffing. People have got to be catching on that something's just not right with me. I don't know what else I can do. If this road doesn't take me to where I want to go, I'm cooked. I've got no other game plan. I need answers—real answers—and quickly. I'm running out of time . . . and rubber cement.*

So, I begin walking on life's path with the motive of Trusting God. This road is definitely less worn than the other one. I have second thoughts every fifty yards or so. But I cannot bring myself to return to the emptiness of the alternative, so I walk on, looking for that second door. Eventually, I spot it, and as I approach it I read the words on the sign above it: Living Out of Who God Says I Am. I tilt my head to the side, thinking the phrase might make more sense if I do. *Those are certainly some words, one right after another. What in the world do they mean? It can't mean what I think it means! When do I get to do something here? Where's the part where I get to prove my sincerity? Where are my guidelines? When do I get to give God my best?* I shake my head and stoop down to read what it says on the doorknob . . . Humility.

Suddenly everything snaps into focus. I've tried so hard, I've supplied all the self-effort the other room demanded, yet received nothing but insecurity and duplicity. I've run out of answers, run out of breath, run out of ability, and so I cry out, *God, if anything good is to come out of this whole deal, you will have to do it. I've tried. I can't. I'm so tired. Please God, you will have to give me the life I am dreaming of. I can't keep doing this anymore. I'm losing confidence that this life in you is even possible. Help me. You must make it happen or I am doomed.* With those words I turn the doorknob.

As I step inside, another hostess immediately approaches. She smiles kindly and, with a voice that is at once knowing and reassuring, says softly, "Welcome to The Room of Grace." I answer tentatively, "Thank . . . you."

She presses, "How are *you?*" The room grows quiet.

Well, I've been here before and so, not to be duped twice, I answer, "I'm fine. Pretty fine . . . Who wants to know?" And the room stays quiet. Gun-shy from the first room, I interpret their silence as judgment, and so I yell out, "All right, listen! I'm *not* fine. I haven't been fine for a long time. I'm tired. I feel guilty, lonely, and depressed. I'm sad most of the time and I can't make my life work. And if any of you knew half my daily thoughts, you'd want me out of your little club. So there, I'm doing *not* fine! Thanks for asking!"

I reach for the doorknob to leave and hear a voice from far back in the crowd. "That's *it?* That's all you've *got?* I'll take your confusion, guilt, and bad thoughts, and I'll raise you compulsive sin and chronic lower back pain! Oh, and I'm in debt up to my ears, and I wouldn't know classical music from a show tune if it jumped up and bit me. You better have more than that puny list if you want to play in my league!"

The greeter smiles and nudges me to say, "I think he means you're welcome here." Emboldened, I smile, and call back, "Do you struggle with forgetting birthdays?" He walks right up to me all the way from the back, puts his hands on my shoulders and says, "Birthdays? I can't remember my *own!*" Everyone in the room laughs the warm laughter of understanding, and I am ushered into the fold of a sweet family of kind and painfully real people. There is not a mask to be seen anywhere.

As I walk further into the room, I notice a huge banner on the back wall. This one reads: Standing with God, with My Sin in Front of Me, Working on It Together. I think, *Wait, this can't be right. How can this be? It sounds presumptuous, careless. Imagining God with his arm around me as we view my sin together? Come on! Surely they've written it down wrong. I've always been told that my sin is still a barrier between God and me. If it could be true that God actually stands with me, in front of my sin, well, that would change everything. If it were true, God has never moved away from me no matter what I've done! Oh my gosh, I'd have to rethink everything.*[2]

Despite my doubts, I can't help but notice that in this room, The Room of Grace, everyone seems vitally alive. The people are obviously imperfect, full of compromise and struggle, but they're authentic enough to talk about it and ask for help. Many have a level of integrity, maturity, love, laughter, freedom, and vitality that I don't recall seeing in the people in the other room. I feel the start of something I haven't felt in . . . well, as long as I can remember. It's safety or something like it. *Toto, I don't think we're in Kansas anymore.*

Where It All Begins

Okay, let's review. Our motives direct what we value and how we act. For example, if we're motivated by money, we will value lucrative careers and people who can help us make money. That value will then shape how we act. It will influence us to pursue certain education, experience, and jobs. We get the word *motion* from *motive*; our motives ultimately determine our actions. God designed us this way.

Motive → Values → Actions

This timeless sequence is at the very heart of the story of the two roads and the two rooms. Our motive as followers of Christ will either keep us in unresolved sin and immaturity or it will free us into God's astonishing life for us. The key to our maturity and freedom lies in the dominant motive that governs our relationship with God. It all starts with motive.

To Trust Him Is to Please Him

Hebrews 11 declares, "And without faith it is impossible to please God."[3] Did you recognize the two paths in this verse? Did you notice that trusting God pleases God? If our primary motive is Pleasing God, we never please him enough and we never learn trust. That's because life on this road is all about my striving, my effort, my ability to make something happen. But if our primary motive is Trusting God, we find out that he is incredibly pleased with us.

So, pleasing God is actually a by-product of trusting God.

But therein lies the problem. We were almost fine with trusting God for the Red Sea deal and the day the sun stood still—but this? Trusting him with *me*! Yikes, that's asking a lot more than we were bargaining for back in the first room. We'd rather work like a dog to keep him almost happy than this absurd thought of trying to trust him with me. Way too much control given away. *Way too much vulnerability. Way too dangerous. Nope, not during my watch.* "Waiter, check please!"

The Deadly Trap

If my life motive is an unwavering determination to Please God,
Then my value will be Striving to Be All God Wants Me to Be,
And my action will be Working on My Sin to Achieve an Intimate Relationship with God.

When we embrace the motive of Pleasing God and live in The Room of Good Intentions, we reduce godliness to this formula:

More right behavior + Less wrong behavior = Godliness

This theology comes with a significant problem: It sets us up to fail and to live in hiddenness. It disregards the godliness — righteousness — that God has already placed in us, at infinite cost,[4] and will sabotage our journey. Once we choose the path of Pleasing God, the bondage of performance persistently badgers us. Our determination to please God traps us in a formula that affixes our masks so tightly that we'll need jackhammers to get them off!

We can never resolve our sin by working on it. Nor can our striving to sin less keep us from future sins. Oh, we may change behaviors for a while, but as we try to hide the sins we can't control, we are unwittingly inviting blame, shame, denial, fear, and anger to become our constant companions. A theology of more right, less wrong behavior creates an environment that gives people permission to wear dozens of disguises and masks. It triggers and complicates the chain reaction of unresolved sin, causing us to lose hope. It keeps us immature! Sin-management theology is breaking our hearts. Yet, even though such harmful thinking has let us down a thousand times, we keep trying to control our bad habits and sin. But we cannot hide the reality of what is true about us, because it comes out in our behavior and gets transferred to all we influence.

The apostle Paul tries to help us think our way out of this trap:

> Have some of you noticed that we are not yet perfect?
> (No great surprise, right?) And are you ready to make
> the accusation that since people like me, who go through
> Christ in order to get things right with God, aren't

perfectly virtuous, Christ must therefore be an accessory to sin? The accusation is frivolous. If I was "trying to be good," I would be rebuilding the same old barn that I tore down. I would be acting as a charlatan.[5]

Many have spent their entire lives serving God, yet they are broken, defeated, lonely, and full of despair. They have embraced a theology of "rebuilding their old barns"; they have placed all their efforts in "trying to be good."

The first son of Adam and Eve, Cain, chose the path of Pleasing God and paid dearly for it. God wanted Cain to acknowledge God's place in his life and to trust God with his intentions. But Cain figured he could make God happy, and that God would make good things happen for him. So Cain worked out a solution on his own terms. He brought offerings that represented his best efforts — the fruit from his fields. Cain was "trying to be good" on his terms. When his offering didn't please God, Cain felt dishonored. He also felt guilt for his sin of disobeying God and offering a self-made sacrifice. Because Cain did not take his sin to God to resolve, it wasn't long before he experienced the Inevitable Effects of his unresolved sin — he became so filled with shame, blame, and anger that he ended up killing his younger brother, Abel.[6]

Early in his reign, King Saul likely struggled with trusting God, just like the Galatians whom Paul corrected. Saul ended up trying to keep God pleased with him. He thought his sacrifice would please God enough to give Saul success against Israel's enemies. But God said, "To obey is better than sacrifice." He knew Saul's obedience would be the evidence of his trust.[7]

Pleasing God is an incredibly good longing. It always will be. But it can't be our primary motivation, or it will imprison our hearts. *Pleasing is not a means to our personal godliness, it is the fruit of our godliness for it is the fruit of trust. We will never please God through our efforts to become godly. Rather, we will only please God—and become godly—when we trust God.* If we strive to please God by solving our sin, we are back at the same insufficient square one that put us in need of a savior. And we are stuck with our talents, skill, desire, ability, longing, chutzpah, diligence, and resolve to make it happen. Now we've got habañera sauce on our cornflakes.

What value, then, flows from the motive of Trusting God? When our motive is Trusting God, our value will be Living Out of Who God Says I Am. Have we already been changed? Yes. As day is from night, we have changed. We have received a new heart, for crying out loud! We have a brand-new core identity. We have already been changed, and now we get to mature into who we already are.[8]

An Identity Too Valuable to Forfeit

God paid an infinite price to buy us back, to redeem us, and to give us a new identity.[9] So, he gets deeply disappointed when we choose not to believe what he says is now true about us. He values our high-priced identity, and he wants us to do the same. How can we show that we value our identity? Please read these words slowly: *By trusting what he says is true about us.*

> If my motive is Trusting God,
>   Then my value will be Living Out of Who God Says I Am,
>   And my action will be Standing with God, with My Sin
>   in Front of Us, Working on It Together.

Nature provides many examples of this incredible discrepancy between who we appear to be and who we truly are. Consider the caterpillar. If we brought a caterpillar to a biologist and asked him to analyze it and describe its DNA, he would tell us, "I know this looks like a caterpillar to you, but scientifically, according to every test, including DNA, this is fully and completely a butterfly." Wow! God has wired into a creature that looks nothing like a butterfly, a perfectly complete butterfly "identity." And because the caterpillar is a butterfly in essence, it will one day display the behavior and attributes of a butterfly. The caterpillar matures into what is already true about it. In the meantime, berating the caterpillar for not being more like a butterfly is not only futile, it will probably hurt his tiny ears!

So it is with us. God has given us the DNA of godliness. We are saints. Righteous. Nothing we do will make us more righteous than we already are. Nothing we do will alter this reality. God knows our DNA. He knows that we are "Christ in me." And now he is asking us to join him in what he knows is true!

Paul asked the Galatian community if they could remember who made this new identity:

> Can't you see the central issue in all this? It is not what you and I do—submit to circumcision, reject circumcision. It is what God is doing, and he is creating something totally new, a free life![10] (emphasis added)

Many of us would answer Paul's question by saying, "No, I can't see the central issue in all this." We actually think that we achieve godliness through striving. We actually think that what we do can "create something totally new." We think we're a match for sin . . . that all we need to do is work a little harder . . . do a little more. We value striving, because we trust our own assessment of who we are instead of God's.[11]

The Great Disconnect

Of course, many people talk as if they have taken the Trusting God road, but in reality they live in The Room of Good Intentions. Why do so many people say the right thing, but then live the wrong life? We call this sweeping reality in the church today The Great Disconnect.

The three stories that follow come from among hundreds that we have been told. We've intentionally selected stories from people employed in Christian work, because if we can see the disconnect between talking and living at this level, we may conclude that this chasm exists everywhere in the body of Christ.

Story one. At a training forum a woman walked up to us in tears and said, "I am very frightened and I don't know what to do, but I have to tell somebody. I am so embarrassed. We are missionaries, with three children, and for over two years, my husband, who is a teacher and executive in our mission, has engaged in major deceit and fraud. He said he wouldn't tell you, but I have to. I cannot live like this any longer."

Question: How can people who move their family to a foreign country to serve God and who rise to leadership positions in their missions and teach truth in scores of situations live in such duplicity? How can what this man believes and teaches others have so little to do with what he actually believes about himself?

Story two. Matthew is a professional counselor. He feels unloved, underappreciated, and lonely. He has been fighting depression for more than five years. He is getting very tired and is losing the strength to keep performing as if everything is okay. But his mask has not worn out to the point where lying is beneath him. Recently he told his organization that he was going on vacation, but the truth was that he was checking himself into a rehab clinic in order to get treatment.

Question: How can a competent Christian counselor deceive

others about his severe need for professional care, while attempting to offer others similar care?

Story three. Doug and Wanda presented a very impressive image of their relationship. They were marriage and family retreat speakers, and he taught future pastors marriage and family courses in a seminary. Yet Doug told us, "I am deeply angry with my wife. I have been for a long time. But my anger is no match for her longstanding disappointment in who I am and have become. She withdraws from me. Our physical relationship is almost nonexistent. We continually speak to scores of couples and families, but we are bluffing about our own marriage."

Question: How can a man and woman with such key responsibilities for transferring truth to others know next to nothing about applying that truth to their own marriage and family? What is likely to happen to those who are being influenced by these kinds of leaders?

Jesus warned us about this very thing when he said: "Be wary of false preachers who smile a lot, dripping with practiced sincerity. . . . Don't be impressed with charisma; look for character. Who preachers *are* is the main thing, not what they say."[12] Erwin McManus catches this fundamental issue when he says, "What I said on Sunday wasn't nearly as important as what I did."[13]

A missionary executive couple, a seasoned counselor, professional teachers and retreat speakers. Each projected a marriage, a life, and a ministry that was "together," healthy. Each can quote Scripture on demand, teach excellent Bible lessons, and instruct others about what it means to be "in Christ." Together they influence thousands who look to them for spiritual direction. Yet, their masked reality tells a very different story about what they really believe about themselves and their circumstances.

Taking the road marked Pleasing God, many, many Christians never understand or live out what it means to be "in Christ Jesus." The

Pleasing God path creates the fearful and hidden environment that produces this disconnect.

These stories demonstrate that our well-crafted, religiously correct words are the least reliable clues about our motives. If we want to determine our real motives, we need to look at our values and actions. In other words, if I:

- Value together-looking, sanitized appearances,
- Value neatly packaged people and can't stand imperfection,
- Act to control my children in public so they'll make me look put together, or
- Camouflage or hide my own unresolved sin from others, then,

I'm motivated by trying to please God . . . and I need everyone else to know that I please God. I feel driven to maintain the appearance of living this God life. It's a motivation everything else must serve.

The New Testament "Gamble"

We discover in The Room of Grace that the almost unthinkable has happened. God has shown all of his cards. He reveals a breathtaking protection that brings us out of hiding. In essence, God says, "What if I tell them who they are? What if I take away any element of fear in condemnation, judgment, or rejection? What if I tell them I love them, will always love them? That I love them right now, no matter what they've done, as much as I love my only Son? That there's nothing they can do to make my love go away?

"What if I tell them there are no lists? What if I tell them I don't keep a log of past offenses, of how little they pray, how often they've let me down, made promises that they don't keep? What if I tell them they are righteous, with my righteousness, right now? What if I tell them they can stop beating themselves up? That they can stop being so formal, stiff, and jumpy around me? What if I tell them I'm *crazy* about them? What if I tell them, even if they run to the ends of the earth and do the most horrible, unthinkable things, that when they come back, I'd receive them with tears and a party?

"What if I tell them that if I am their Savior, they're going to heaven no matter what—it's a done deal? What if I tell them they have a new nature—saints, not saved sinners who should now 'buck-up and be better if they were any kind of Christians, after all he's done for you!' What if I tell them that I actually live in them now? That I've put my love, power, and nature inside of them, at their disposal? What if I tell them that they don't have to put on a mask? That it is ok to be who they are at this moment, with all their junk. That they don't need to pretend about how close we are, how much they pray or don't, how much Bible they read or don't. What if they knew they don't have to look over their shoulder for fear if things get too good, the other shoe's gonna drop?

"What if they knew I will never, ever use the word *punish* in relation to them? What if they knew that when they mess up, I will never "get back at them?" What if they were convinced that bad circumstances aren't my way of evening the score for taking advantage of me? What if they knew the basis of our friendship isn't how little they sin, but how much they let me love them? What if I tell them they can hurt my heart, but that I never hurt theirs? What if I tell them I like Eric Clapton's music too? What if I tell them I never really liked the Christmas handbell deal with the white gloves? What if I tell them they can open their eyes when they pray and still go to heaven? What if I tell them there is no secret agenda, no trapdoor? What if I tell them it isn't about their self-effort, but about allowing me to live my life through them?"

When you stand at the crossroads, you decide which road to choose largely upon how you see God's "gamble." *Do I really believe this stuff will hold up—for me?* This is the way of life in The Room of Grace. It is the way home to healing, joy, peace, fulfillment, contentment, and release into God's dreams for us. It almost feels like we're stealing silverware from the king's house, doesn't it? Truth is, the king paid a lot so that you wouldn't have to try to steal any silverware. He gets to give it to you; and other stuff so big and good and beautiful that we couldn't even begin to stuff it into our bag of loot. Wow! It takes the eyes some adjustment to look into such light, huh?

Changing or Maturing?

If we refuse to enter The Room of Grace, we will constantly be striving in The Room of Good Intentions. We will strive to change into something we are not yet: godly. In The Room of Grace we grow up and mature into something that is already true about us: godly. The first room creates a works-based, performance-driven relationship with God and puts the responsibility on our resources. The second room places the responsibility on the resources of God.

God is not interested in changing you. He already has. The new DNA is set. God wants you to believe that he has already changed you so that he can get on with the process of maturing you into who you already are. Trust opens the way for this process—for God to bring you to maturity. If you do not trust God, you can't mature, because your focus is messed up. You're still trying to change enough to be labeled godly.

> Does the God who lavishly provides you with his own presence, his Holy Spirit, working things in your lives you could never do for yourselves, does he do these things because of your strenuous moral striving or because you trust him to do them in you?[14]

If you are living in The Room of Grace, you aren't making desperate attempts to improve yourself. You know you cannot change yourself; you can only mature because of who you already are: a spiritually new creation born of the Spirit, a saint maturing into the image of Christ.

Those inside The Room of Grace place their effort just where God can use it. Ponder the contrast of how Effort works in the two rooms. On the road of Pleasing God, Effort gets me into The Room of Good Intentions. On the road of Trusting God, Effort is found inside The Room of Grace. Effort is never a means of pleasing God or getting God's grace or changing myself. Effort is a response that God uses to work together with me on my sin, to mature into that person with whom he is already pleased. Effort born out of striving to please God never ceases to tire us. Effort born out of resting in his pleasure never ceases to renew us.

Pleasing God with the Right Motive

Pleasing God is a wonderful desire, but it never gives entry to The Room of Grace. Now, inside The Room of Grace, we finally can honor our yearning to please God.

When we reverse trusting and pleasing, it's like switching "trust and obey" to "obey and trust." Placing obedience before trust locks us into a mindset of obeying to please God, to earn his favor, his pleasure.

If we do not start with trusting who God says we are, we will end up trusting in our own resources to try to please God. This kind of self-sufficient mindset nauseates God.[15]

The following statements do not gain us entry into The Room of Grace; they describe the privilege and fulfillment of living in it.

- "Live a life worthy of the Lord [that you] may please him in every way."[16]
- "Offer your bodies as living sacrifices, holy and pleasing to

God."[17]

- "The gifts you sent . . . are an acceptable sacrifice, pleasing to God."[18]
- "Live in order to please God, as in fact you are living."[19]

Now, we have pleasing in its proper place. The citizens in The Room of Grace get the privilege of experiencing the pleasure of God, because they have pleased God by trusting him.

The Goal of Life

John still remembers sitting down with Bill more than eighteen years ago when Bill was his boss. John was a young, gifted preacher, complete with four years of seminary, a snappy briefcase, and a bookshelf full of impressive-looking, scholarly books. He told Bill, "I think there are about two or three issues that I haven't yet overcome. They're not too complex or difficult. Once they get solved I really think I can be used by God in a big way."

John expected Bill to respond, "Well, let's get to work on those. What are they? Let's look at them one at a time and solve them so you can really take off." Instead Bill looked at John for a long time and then slowly said the words to John that God has used to change the entire focus of how he lives the Christian life. "John, then I hope that you never, ever completely solve those issues. You will become self-dependent. You will become self-sufficient. The goal is not for you to get all of your 'stuff' solved. You never will. There is an endless list of stuff. God is gracious to reveal only a snippet at a time. The goal is to learn to depend on—to trust—what God says is true about you, so that together you can begin dealing with that stuff."

John was headed straight for The Room of Good Intentions where The Great Disconnect spreads like a viral bug. Worse, the Pleasing

God path John intended to travel would have produced two or three hundred more unresolved sin issues. But John learned about a road less traveled by. And that has made all the difference.

If you have been searching for the hope described in this chapter, come with us further into The Room of Grace. Discover how God's power to handle sin in this environment of grace not only resolves sin, but also allows God to do in us far beyond what we could even ask or imagine.[20]

─≡ DID YOU DISCOVER?

- Pleasing God and Trusting God represent the ultimate motives of our hearts.

- If my life motive is an unwavering determination to Please God
    Then my value will be Striving to Be All God Wants Me to Be
        And my action will be Working on My Sin to Achieve an Intimate Relationship with God.

- When we strive to sin less, we don't sin less.

- Pleasing God is an incredibly good longing. It always will be. It just can't be our primary motivation, or it will imprison our hearts.

- If my motive is Trusting God
    Then my value will be Living Out of Who God Says I Am
        And my action will be Standing with God, with My Sin in Front of Us, Working on It Together.

- Many people say they have taken the path of Trusting God but have ended up in The Room of Good Intentions. This is called The Great Disconnect.

- Our response to the New Testament "gamble" becomes a limitless test—telling us which road we've chosen.

- God is not interested in changing the Christian. He already has.

- Trust opens the way for God to bring us to maturity. If we do not trust, we do not mature.

- If we do not start with trusting who God says we are, we will end up with trusting in our own resources to try to please God.

CHAPTER THREE

Grace Works!

The interpretation of grace as having only to do with guilt is utterly false to biblical teaching and renders spiritual life in Christ unintelligible.

— Dallas Willard

Every week we work with Mark, a gifted analyst and a high-capacity problem solver. As a teen, Mark became an Eagle Scout. Later he received an MBA and managed people and projects in the technology sector. Mark trusted Christ when he was a sophomore in college. From that time on, all he wanted to do was please God, to "sell out" for God, to study the Bible, to serve God anywhere in the world. Most of all, Mark wanted to get rid of the sin issues that plagued him.

In time, Mark left the business world to serve in a mission organization. We asked him to describe his life on the path of Pleasing God and his life on the path of Trusting God.

> When I came to Christ as an adult, I was desperate to turn my life around. I did anything and everything I was told to do in order to get rid of my sin issues—forgive, repent, memorize, meditate, pray, serve, fellowship, disciple, commit, commit again. But my issues remained and even compounded. Before I came to Jesus I felt discounted in relationship after relationship. My own

mother disowned me. My deep hurt caused me to believe that no matter how hard I tried, I would still be worthless—and I continued to believe this as a Christian. My own sin and the sin of others against me prevented me from even understanding what it really meant that I had a new identity—but I was sure trying to get one.

In my fervor, I could trust God for cities, countries, nations, for thousands to accept Christ, but I could not trust God with me. I did not see myself as godly; I saw myself as valiantly trying to become godly. I was ready for martyrdom, to live among any tribe, but I could not live with who I was. I was a failure, doing my best to break out of my junk and hiddenness.

Over time, the effects of past sins became worse than the actual sins against me. I had become an angry, bitter man, ashamed of who I was. This mindset adversely pervaded every relationship. Simultaneously, I wanted to please God, so I was daily striving to do 110 percent for him, serving him like crazy, and getting kudos from others for doing so. I was a mess.

Then my wife and I met up with some people who actually valued others with issues—issues like mine. This was a place where people were safe to share their struggles, their painful pasts, and their present issues. This was a community of grace, where the truth of my identity would eventually become fog-free for me. I would actually begin to believe who God says I am. They actually believed I was, by God's grace, a saint. Me, a saint! They believed I had a new identity, just like theirs. This enabled me once again to get in touch with the same gift of trust God gave me when I came to know Jesus. I would begin to trust God and others with me. During those years I began to experience what I call "Spiritual Teflon." The untruths, sin issues, and the striving gradually started sliding off of me. The truth started sticking as I learned to trust.

I am a very different man, husband, father, and colleague than I was eight years ago. I am living out of who I am in Christ, not who others have declared me to be in times past. I am loving more and sinning less. I am influencing people's lives in ways that previously I could not even imagine. I am living an exhilarating life—I am living the Father's dreams for me, his very well-loved child. Trusting God's view of me has been the most intense, most difficult, and most comprehensive maturing and releasing process I have ever experienced.

Thousands have experienced the trauma and sadness reflected in the first part of Mark's story, and they long to experience the second half. They actually can. Explore The Room of Grace with us to see how grace works.

How Does Grace Work?

How does grace resolve our sin issues? These five truths of grace give us lasting answers for this question:
1. Humility attracts grace.
2. Grace changes our life focus.
3. Grace lets God handle sin.
4. Grace melts masks.
5. Grace changes how we treat each other and our sin issues.

Attracting God's Grace Through Humility

When we turn the knob of Humility, we walk right into The Room of Grace. Like a mutual friend introducing us to our future spouse, humility escorts us to grace.

Humility requires trust. It is her core feature. Humility believes that I can trust God to teach, direct, and protect me. Humility also believes that God has provided others in my life to do the same. In this case, I am depending on God to tell me how the world looks and works, giving up my rights to notions I had before. I am "leaning into" his evaluation of reality, one I did not previously have or know. This is why we define humility as *trusting God and others with me.*

Recall that God resists the proud, but gives grace to the humble.[1] So, if a relationship or community lacks grace, that relationship or community is low on trust. One simply cannot nurture a realm of grace without trust. I can enter The Room of Grace only when I humbly acknowledge that I need to trust God and others with myself and give up my striving to be godly.

In 1 Peter 5 and elsewhere in Scripture we learn that grace can never be earned, but it can be spurned through untrust, the absence of humility. We never deserve grace—it is always unmerited—but we can invite grace into our lives, we can attract it. How? By trusting God. God gives his grace to those who trust him—to the humble.[2] Trust, humility, and grace guide us into an astonishing life.

We sometimes fool ourselves by thinking we are being humble when we see ourselves in all our failure and repugnancy. We think God is pleased with our self-belittling: "O God, I am lower than sludge clinging to a rock in the deepest part of the sea, which receiving no light, causes all near to wonder if it exists at all. I am and shall remain the pitiful chorus of a hollow dirge, fit only for the recounting of what might have been."

Many people in The Room of Good Intentions think it is somehow pious to present themselves to God in this way. It is their way of proving that they are not proud. But their inaccurate self-deprecation proves just the opposite.

Indeed, in God's eyes this behavior exhibits not humility, but pride. Why? Because we are trusting our own assessment of ourselves and taking credit for our relative goodness. We are denying God's longing to be our goodness, our power, our ability, our strength, our healing, and our truth. That's why grace is in such short supply in The Room of Good Intentions. Pride shuts grace down. In contrast, humility allows us to boldly trust how God sees us, and it ushers us into this amazing room that specializes in resolving our sin, maturing us, and freeing us into God's destiny for us.

Back to our question: How does God in the realm of grace actually resolve my sin issues? The environment of grace provides me with truth, acceptance, healing, safety, perspective, freedom,[3] and power that I did not before know; these realities are foundational to resolving my sin issues. Conversely, prideful striving in The Room of Good Intentions sucks grace—and therefore power—right out of the room. That's the huge difference between the rooms. Our friend Mark did not know God's power until he gave up on his own power, which was no power at all.[4]

This shift revealed God's grace to Mark, which led him to the second insight: A healthy response to the question, Who am I? is "I am a person *already* deeply pleasing to God."

Grace Changes Our Life Focus

When we became Christians, something happened that actually changed who we are. Most of us would say, "Yeah, that's true. I believe that." If so, then why do so many of us slog on through life with unresolved sin issues? "Well, um, I guess, well, um . . . well, I'm not sure I know."

Consider this diagram. In this life, we who have trusted Christ will always have sin issues, and we will always have the identity God gave us. They are constants. Unchanging realities.

Working on My Sin Issues
⟶

Trusting Who God Says I Am
⟶

It's key that we ask ourselves: Which one of these two constants defines my life focus? Which offers me the hope of experiencing the other? If we opt for the top line, we will never experience the bottom line. But, if we focus on the bottom line, we will experience unparalleled transformation regarding our sin issues. It's a whole new way of seeing, not unlike those pictures popular a few years ago. At first glance you just saw patterns. But if you squinted and looked more intensely, you eventually saw shapes in three dimensions, revealing a beautiful and astounding picture. The first time you broke through to see such images was truly a remarkable moment. It is the same with seeing all the way through the patterns of our sin issues into the beautiful and astounding reality of who God says we are. Suddenly life is in three dimensions—alive, rich, and full of hope.

Do you see why the path of Trusting God is so important? We will never know our identity in Christ—and we will never live out of our identity—unless we start on the path of Trusting God. To resolve our sin issues we must begin trusting who God says we are. If our life focus is the top line, if we strive to eradicate our sin issues so we can somehow create a "new me" or "changed me," we will always keep "me" bound to "my sin" and we will remain immature. Trusting Who God Says I Am lays the foundation for maturity.

Many of us say we believe that salvation brings a "new birth," a new identity, but the way we view ourselves betrays our words; we don't believe its reality in us for a second. Instead we think we must keep striving to become someone who will be better. And all along we deny the mind-boggling truth that we have already become that someone.[5] In the last chapter, we called this gap between who we say we are and who we actually believe we are The Great Disconnect. It is the reason why the three of us teach that, "How I view myself is the most revealing commentary of my theology."

- It tells me about my relationship with God.
- It tells me about my relationship with others.
- It tells me whether my trust is in myself or in God.
- It tells me if I am maturing into Christ's likeness.

Letting God Handle My Sin

Many Christians know God loves us and wants to be with us, but we also believe our sin has put an impossible mass between God and us. We understand that Jesus has made a way for us to one day be together in heaven, but right now—until we get better, do better, or start to take things seriously—we believe we'll have to settle for rare moments of intimacy with him. We know ourselves too well, and there is no way we're ever going to be able to keep from sinning. We believe God loves us, but we also believe he's pretty disappointed with us. We expect to see him someday, but for now we can only hope that some days we will feel his touch on our lives. That's as good as it gets on this earth . . . or so we've come to believe.

Here's another way of putting it. Imagine a lake, maybe one hundred yards across and so wide you can't see a way around in either direction. On the other side stands someone you long to see. But you can't walk around the lake because bushes bristling with thorns and needles cover its banks. To complicate things even further, the lake water is so polluted and full of poisonous snakes and amphibious eels that it's not safe to wade in, let alone swim. You have no boat and none is in sight. What do you do? You yell back and forth across the lake in a deeply unsatisfying relationship.

The lake represents your sin, and the person on the other side of the lake is God, whom you want to be close to more than anything else in the world. Question: How do you get to him? Answer: You don't. Not unless you can find some way to remove the sin from your life. But you've got a small problem—you are pouring more sin into the lake every day.

Thousands of people heard an illustration something like this just before they asked Jesus to save them. It's an accurate picture of someone who doesn't have life in Christ, but the illustration makes no sense for the Christian. So why do thousands of Christians, now possessing the righteousness of God, live as if this illustration still depicts their relationship with God? They feel distant from God, imagining that a pile of sin separates them. It's as if their salvation never took place.

Ironically, striving to achieve this relationship with the Father will keep us in unresolved sin and immaturity. It produces just the opposite of what we're working for! People in The Room of Good Intentions hold this view. There, piles of sin separate each person from God, who is on the other side of the pile. Supposedly, moral striving will save the day, so everyone in the room keeps trying to chip away at that mound, all the while realizing they're creating a bigger pile. Then, every time they manage to change a behavior or not succumb to a poor choice, they think they have accomplished something big. This process breeds pride, not humility; sin, not maturity.

Sin will not be managed. Behavior change and sin management are deceptively tricky boxing opponents. We win some early rounds. This increases our confidence and by the fifth or sixth round, we break into a rendition of the Ali Shuffle. *Hey, this isn't so hard.* Soon, we're mugging for the cameras . . . and the next thing we know, we're on the canvas, knocked into another world by a devastating left hook.

Our efforts will not make us godly. Such thinking winks at sin. Moral striving to become godly only keeps us slaves to sin.[6] Our friend Mark lived under this enslavement until he chose to let God handle his sin. He was like thousands of Christians whose life motive prevents them from living out of their new identity, who think, *If I just add this to that and that to the other thing, and keep all the dishes spinning, I'll get there!* Do you see the futility of this thinking? If the only thing we received by Christ's atoning death was a "get out of hell" card, then we have no hope of living a life worth living. Our life is as bleak as it was before we ever came to know him.

Grace teaches us to trust that God can handle our sin, and only God. Our thoughts begin to run like this: *I can't handle my sin. I can't save myself. I can't change myself. Thank you, God, for already making me godly, so you could stand with me, ready to address my sin out there in front of us. Lord, thank you there is no pile of sin and junk between us. If there were, I wouldn't stand a chance of intimacy with you. I know I can't survive away from you. Once, I thought that this particular sin would fulfill and satisfy me. But, Father, as we look at it together, I am learning to trust your assessment of what will satisfy me. So, what do you want us to do about this sin? I am not going to try to manage it or throw it to the ground. I trust you for the next step.*

This heart-set changes our entire approach to sin, for only in The Room of Grace do we take sin seriously. In the Room of Good Intentions we may talk a good game, but we actually take sin less seriously as we marshal our effort and ability to do something about our sin. Our ability to resolve our sin plus $3.35 will only get us a tall latte in a paper cup. Ah, but in The Room of Grace, Jesus Christ is honored, depended upon, and submitted to for the resolution of our sin issues. His sacrificial death on a cross remains our only solution, not only for eternal life, but for every sin we've committed or received from another. This trust acknowledges the seriousness of our sin, for it properly weakens our dependency on our own abilities while strengthening our dependency on that which can truly defeat the power of sin. Now when we mess up, we can say, "Lord, this sin doesn't surprise me a bit. I hate that I am prone to sin. I am practiced. I expect that kind of thinking to trip me up at times. As a matter of fact, I can't even handle that sin, and on my own I can't even stop that sin. That's how powerful I believe sin is. I need you now."

Do you really think God would make it so hard to live a life that pleases him? What if we didn't have to work so hard? What if our sin doesn't affect how close we are to God? What if God meant it when he said, "I will never leave you nor forsake you"?[7] What if God, knowing that we don't have the power to address our sin, could walk around that impossible mass and right up to us? What if he could put his arm around us and enjoy us right now—no matter how much unresolved sin we have in our life? What if we could both stand together, looking at "my" sin, not for the sake of condemnation, but to solve it together? What if we took responsibility for the fact that we are the ones who sinned, and then with God at our side turn to trust his provision for the very sin that we've just committed? What if we truly believed we were without condemnation?[8] What if grace was that strong?

Welcome to life in The Room of Grace! Amazingly, the more we depend upon Jesus and his full ability to heal the effects of our sin, the less we sin! Now, that, friend, is like eating the grande Mexican sampler and losing weight at the same time!

Grace Melts Masks
Striving leaves us dysfunctional and immature because it creates hiddenness. Masks abound in The Room of Good Intentions. It is the world of false appearances. Hiddenness makes us vulnerable to sin

and thwarts maturity. It breeds compulsive sinning.

In contrast, an environment of grace is full of light—not darkness. Grace creates authenticity. Why is that important? Because authenticity melts masks, and reveals our true face.

The community of grace begins to break the cycle of sin issues that have kept us bound. Remember, Mark said, "I began to experience what I call 'Spiritual Teflon' in this environment of grace. The untruths, sin issues, and the striving gradually started sliding off me. The truth started sticking as I learned to trust."

How can we explain an environment of grace? It's like cool water gushing from an oversized garden hose on a hot summer day. It just keeps making us laugh with delight as it knocks us over, again and again.

Many of us understand grace as a theological position. And it is delightfully that. Undeserved, unending, unearned, unwavering, grace is God's inexhaustible love and absolute acceptance of us, coupled with his unabashed delight in us. Grace brings us adoption into God's family, a new identity, a new life, new power, new capacity, and God's full protection—with absolutely no strings attached!

But grace is much more than a theological position. Equally and simultaneously, grace is an actual environment, a realm, a present-tense reality that weaves around and through every moment of even our worst day. God's gift of grace continuously and always surrounds us. When we "approach the throne of grace,"[9] we are not coming to a throne made out of grace. The triune God lives in the realm of grace. Jesus, who lived on this earth, came full of grace and truth.[10]

Like any atmosphere, an environment of grace contains intangible, yet detectable, qualities. In this book we are explaining the particles that make up this atmosphere. You may not be able to see them—but you sure can feel them, just as you can detect whether you are breathing the air of a pine-filled forest or a smog-filled city. What a difference grace makes!

Trusting God means trusting that such a realm exists.

You may have experienced grace as an environment in a counseling room. Many individuals who cannot detect a grace environment in their churches or organizations are referred to counselors. These counselors often provide safety, acceptance, and hope that we may not have sensed in our everyday environment. If this has been your experience, then you understand how grace works in an environment, in a relationship. And, you probably experienced a life-changing season, because grace environments help us mature.

God does not ask us to get our act together or to stop sinning so much before we can enjoy this realm. God wants only one thing from us: He wants us to become more dependent upon him. He wants us to walk on the path of Trusting God, where we can begin interacting with others on the journey. When someone shows grace to us, that person begins cultivating an environment that reflects God's grace. It is an authentic, unhidden place, where our masks start melting, our sin can be known—and, therefore, addressed with the power of grace. Such places liberate the soul and change people like Mark . . . and our friend Graeme:

> By my early thirties, the thorns Christ talks about in the parable of the sower—the worries and pleasures and riches of this life—had reduced my heart's desire for Christ to a dim flicker. What caused my spiritual anesthesia? I had discovered it was easy to play the fool.
>
> Without the principles of truth and grace, practiced in relationship, the only guide I had to putting my life together was to mimic a pattern or a format or a style—somebody else's program for a successful journey with God. It got me performing my way to God, and he

wasn't impressed. Then I encountered some people who showed me grace. Solomon said there is nothing new under the sun, but an environment of grace was new to me. The truths about how God sees me and who I am in Christ came roaring into my life.

I discovered that if these truths are trusted, they infect everything. They're the foundation for my marriage, how I deal with my kids, how I do ministry, live life, and how I work as a lawyer.

Blaise Pascal sewed into his coat a piece of paper with these words on it: "Fire, God of Abraham, God of Isaac, God of Jacob, not of the philosophers and scholars. Certainty. Heartfelt joy. Peace. God of Jesus Christ. Joy, joy, joy, oceans of joy." Ten years ago I would have envied him. Today, I join him.

Grace Changes How We Treat Each Other When We Sin

When we live in The Room of Grace, we begin to relate to others differently. We begin to experience true intimacy. Do you know why? For the same reason we no longer have distance between God and us. Grace wonderfully reorients all our relationships.[11]

We no longer see one another with our sin between us. We no longer see one another through the grid of our shame, blame, and anger. We no longer feel we must compete with each other. We no longer come to our relationships feeling ashamed, condemned, and unacceptable. We no longer hide our real faces from each other. We begin to discover that our character is actually formed in relationships. We stand in front of each other, true-faced. Safety, protection, and love characterize the relationships in this room rather than mistrust, deceit, and guardedness.

We see one another as saints who sin, rather than as sinners who are saved. If we truly believe in our heart of hearts that we are saints, then we're able to stand with each other in the reality of our sin. But if we don't believe that, and instead view each other as sinners, we will demand that others work on their sin in order to have a relationship with us. Naturally, we will be tempted to hide our sin from one another. We cannot divorce how we view ourselves and our sin from how we view others. If we think, *My sin is between God and me*, then we will also think, *Your sin and my sin stand between us*. And we will make the same mistake of striving to work on our sin so we can have a better, closer relationship. Not only do we continue to sin, but we also feel even further from God and too tired to enjoy him even if we could! We'd almost be better off to ignore the sin and go fishing. At least we might catch a fish.

After connecting with this truth of grace for the first time, two men walked up to Bill. Ryan said, "I have known my friend Sam here for many, many years. We have a deep relationship. Over lunch we did the exercise that encourages us to choose to believe that we are each saints. During that exercise I learned something about Sam that he has kept hidden from me all this time." Ryan then turned to Sam and said, "Why don't you share with Bill what you just told me."

Sam said, "I told Ryan that once, a long time ago, I acted out in unhealthy behavior, and that I am presently tempted to do so again. In fact, I just wish someone would hit on me."

When Sam finished, Ryan said, "Not long ago, if you would have told me what you told me today, I would have rejected you, Sam. I would have pulled away from you. Today I cannot do that because I know you are a saint and my brother. I don't understand why all the stuff you told me is true. I feel deceived. You've lied to me for many years. I feel hurt and confused. I have a thousand questions and I don't have a clue how to help you with what you just told me. But, Sam,

I can tell you that I am proud of you for telling me. And I will stand together with you, because I know who you are. You are a saint, Sam. You are a saint with some pretty deep issues that are freaking me out at this particular moment. But you are my brother. I will not walk away from you."

When our theology gives us permission to see Christians as sinners, we give ourselves permission to reject them. But Ryan saw his friend for who he was—a saint. So he could literally put his arm around Sam and weep over the reality of what was true. Ryan didn't send his friend away to deal with his sin. He intentionally walked with him into God's resolution. That's what God models and teaches us to do in The Room of Grace.

For years, these two men had seen each other only as saved sinners. They were terrified to disclose what was true in their lives. They instinctively knew they were viewed as sinners first and would receive the condemnation of a sinner. Now the spell had been broken. Sam had disclosed a significant area of struggle in his life, and both were seeing each other as dearly accepted saints who were also fragile and compromised.

When we trust God, we live by this value: *The godly are those who trust God with themselves.* Period. Sounds like Hebrews 11, doesn't it? The godly ones are those who live by faith (trust). Sounds like Romans 3, doesn't it?

Grace's permission radically changes how we see each other and how we deal with sin. We can now be exactly who we are, with all our issues and problems and unresolved stuff, and still fully experience grace, love, and acceptance. This single reality is perhaps the greatest feeling in this room. It resolves sin issues. This room has no caste system. No superstars or pretenders. Flawed and broken and fragile people are celebrated for their vulnerability and dogged dependence upon their identity in Christ.

As we begin to believe these truths, we become the kind of safe place for others in The Room of Grace that J. R. R. Tolkien describes in *The Fellowship of the Ring.* "Frodo was now safe. . . . The house was, as Bilbo had long ago reported, 'a perfect house, whether you like food or sleep or storytelling or singing, or just sitting and thinking best, or a pleasant mixture of them all.' Merely to be there was a cure for weariness, fear and sadness."[12]

The Ultimate Goal

Some of you briefly caught sight of a streak of light flashing through The Room of Grace. Hope awakened. Wonder stirred in you. Yet, you struggle to describe the splendor you sensed. The sensation we believe you felt is this: Resolving sin is only the *starting point* of life in The Room of Grace. God's final objective for us is not resolving sin or "getting well." God's ultimate goal is maturing us into who he says we are, and then releasing us into the dreams he designed for us before the world began.[13] That's where all of this is going. That's what has awakened your hope. When we swim in the ocean of God's grace, we can't help but respond with playful abandon. We will grin, laugh, and splash around. We will burst into song at inappropriate times, dance, play, serve, fall on our knees in worship, give our lives away, and embrace each other. We'll sin less. We'll love more. We are free.[14] And, we'll naturally think about others. We'll sacrifice to reach to the lonely, the lost, the helpless, the forgotten. Everything, everything seems fresh, vibrant—alive. We find ourselves pausing in the middle of a busy day, shaking our heads and whispering, "Go figure . . . me."

Astonishment fills Mark and Graeme's stories, in part, because in their maturing they began influencing others beyond what they could have imagined. God carefully designed his "influence system" so that we would have to influence far more out of who we are than what we do.[15] Therefore, God's "influence system" requires personal maturity. Do you see why God so deeply wants us to mature into the "likeness of his Son"?[16] There is no profound influence without it.

Note well this sequence of truths:

- We cannot profoundly influence others without maturing.
- We cannot mature without finding resolution to our sin issues.
- We cannot find resolution to our sin issues without trusting who God says we are.

As we live out this cluster of truths, our life will illustrate that the ultimate goal of grace is not resolving our sin, because maturing and destiny are the endgame. God's dreams for us are the ultimate goal.

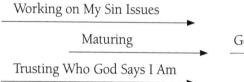

Experiencing the Ultimate Life

Our friend Cary is living this astonishing life. He recently celebrated his fortieth birthday. His wife threw a surprise party for him and invited dozens of his closest friends. Cary came into faith with several dozen addictions, compulsions, dysfunctions, and twisted family dynamics. He's been a Christian for several decades, and yet he still struggles with the effects of all that junk. Cary is not "fixed." It's likely he will struggle with significant issues for the rest of his days on earth. But Cary is healthy and resolving the sin issues in his life. He believes in his identity and, as a result, is doing profound stuff for God's glory, because he came to trust God's assessment of him, even in the middle of pain.

Despite Cary's "failure" to get his whole act together, almost every person at that party stood up and spoke of the countless ways Cary had been used in their lives. There were many tears, long hugs, and heartfelt affirmations of how caring and important a friend he had been to each of them. The sharing must have lasted two hours! Anyone watching would have concluded that Cary is a significant minister to that community. The following week, Cary dropped off some chairs at John's house and told him, "You know I am meeting with a counselor. I told her about the birthday party last weekend, the affirmation, and all the things others said were true about me, in spite of all the junk I know is in me. And she said to me, 'You are one of the truly lucky ones. Very few have this life you have been given. I envy you.' She said she envied *me!*"

John looked long and hard into the face of this man he'd been through so much with and said, "Cary, you prove the penalties of being messed up every day in new and exciting ways. But you have come to believe who you are in Christ. And so you are not sick, but healthy. And there are about a hundred of us who are deeply privileged to know you, because knowing you has made us better people."

At the start of the book we said that God's dreams are not ultimately so much about you. Cary could never, in his wildest imagination, see a day when he would be anything but a drain on anyone who got stuck with him. But God's dream for Cary was not just to give him a safe place, or a place where he could be healed, or even a place where he could be loved and known. God's ultimate dream for Cary is that he will bring significant beauty into the lives of others. That's what The Room of Grace ultimately prepares us for. The fragile, the goofed up, the compromised, the inadequate, the failed, the squirrelly, those full of pain and despair, even the arrogant and the controlling—all mature into health when they enter into this room. And these—oh yes these—they get to minister hope and beauty and healing in the kingdom where the humble, even with their warts and boils, become a healing balm.

Remaining in The Room of Grace

This Room of Grace, you see, is tricky business for those who've believed that self-made excellence makes the man. That's why some don't stay once they come in. For not only must you believe that *you* are accepted, you must learn to accept the yokels already here and who come in fresh each week! They're goofy, flawed, common, odd, broken, weird, and often inappropriate. Oh, every now and then some presentable people slip in, but it soon becomes obvious to everyone that their "presentableness" is only a mask. They, too, must learn to rest in the sufficiency of Christ in them or they'll soon go back to a familiar crowd in The Room of Good Intentions.

On the other hand, when you think you don't belong, when you believe you are too failed, too unfit, or can't live among this band of rabble without a mask, the others in The Room of Grace will, each in their own way, say to you, "That's all you got?" It will be their way of saying to you, "You are welcome here."

Do you see how The Room of Grace helps people trust who God says they are and then deal with sin in a new way that enables them to mature? Grace allows them to strip away the veneer and trust God with their sin, their healing, and their growth. They are vulnerable people who rely on God's strength in the midst of their often-compromised existence. It is breathtaking to behold.

Do you have a Room of Grace where you live? If not, here's hope: You can begin creating such a room, even if it's just with one other person. Remember, the power is not in a ready-made room that you somehow stumble into; the power is in the grace. It's God's grace, and you can attract his grace all by yourself—through a humble heart. He loves to give excessive amounts of grace to humble people. Trust God and others with you, and see if this room doesn't start taking shape right before your eyes.

Getting to the Payoff

Many of us may not think much about our influence on others, because unresolved sin keeps us immature and thinking mostly about ourselves. We come to Christ "me-centered," and we struggle to progress beyond that condition. The wonderful dreams God has for us often remain unclear because unresolved sin issues block our view. In our immaturity we may even think that our dreams for ourselves are more significant than what God has planned for us.

God thinks about our influence on others all the time. He designed us to influence others.[17] And, every so often, we catch a glimpse of the destiny God has planned for us, and new longings stir within. We fill up with fresh motivation to learn how grace works and to follow God's voice into a land of adventure and fulfillment. Then we struggle to remember the entry point to that great land. It's like standing outside the bakery, face pressed against the window, smelling the fresh bread and pastries inside, but we can't locate the door to get inside, where we would surely sample every wonderful treat in those glass cases. Remember the door to the "bakery"? It's the door that teaches us how to live out of who God says we are by turning the doorknob of Humility, and stepping into The Room of Grace.

We need to tell you one more thing that you can look forward to in The Room of Grace: You will receive gifts there, gifts for every occasion and every need. Jesus passes them out for the asking, to meet specific needs. God has three gifts created specifically to heal your wounds and resolve your sin. Gifts essential for maturing you and giving you the desires of your heart.[18]

In the next three chapters, you'll encounter God's powerful grace gifts of love, repentance, and forgiveness. You'll see how grace actually changes how you apply these truths in resolving sin and maturing the real you. So, here's to your true face, a face that, with increasing brilliance, reflects the majesty of our great God.[19] It might almost seem too good to be true, but it's not a fantasy, it's a reality.

─≡ DID YOU DISCOVER?

- These five truths of grace give us lasting answers for resolving our sin issues:

  - Humility attracts grace.

  - Grace changes my life focus.

  - Grace lets God handle sin.

  - Grace melts masks.

  - Grace changes how we treat each other and our sin issues.

- We define humility as trusting God and others with me. Therefore, if a community lacks grace, that community is low on trust.

- Pride shuts down grace.

- The environment of grace provides me with truth, acceptance, healing, safety, perspective, freedom, and power that I did not before know. These realities are foundational to resolving my sin issues.

- Trusting Who God Says I Am lays the foundation for maturity.

- How I view myself is the most revealing commentary of my theology.

- Striving leaves us dysfunctional and immature because it creates hiddenness.

- Grace creates authenticity. Authenticity melts masks.

- Safety, protection, and love characterize relationships in The Room of Grace, rather than mistrust, deceit, and guardedness. We stand in front of each other, true-faced.

- We need to see one another as saints who sin, rather than as sinners who are saved.

- When our theology gives us permission to see Christians as sinners, we give ourselves permission to reject them.

- God's final objective for us is not resolving sin or "getting well." God's ultimate goal is maturing us into who he says we are and releasing us into the dreams he designed for us before the world began.

- God carefully designed his "influence system" so that we would have to influence far more out of who we are than what we do.

- We cannot profoundly influence others, without maturing.

- We cannot mature without finding resolution to our sin issues.

- We cannot find resolution to our sin issues without trusting who God says we are.

CHAPTER FOUR

The Supreme Gift of Grace: Love

Grace is the face that love wears, when it meets imperfection.
—Joseph R. Cooke

You may be deeply encouraged by the last two chapters and at the same time feel somewhat depressed. You may be thinking: *Why didn't I learn this stuff earlier? I now realize I missed out on that second room I should have entered long ago. Wasted years spent in The Room of Good Intentions affixed my mask so tightly that it is now really hard to take off. My time there gave me scars I fear I will always carry.*

For you, here is really, really good news. When you enter The Room of Grace, Jesus has some gifts for you. Gifts for every occasion and every need. They are given for the asking, to meet your specific needs. For every issue, every unresolved sin, every wound, God has created a gift specifically to meet that need, resolve that sin, and heal that wound.

In the middle of our misery, Jesus taps us on the shoulder and says, "I have something for you that cost me everything to get for you. Here, it's a gift of my grace for you." Written across the gift is one word: love. The attached card reads: "Take it, apply it, and trust me to make it real. I love you. Jesus."

Love, the first gift of grace, acts as a solvent to lift our masks. It acts as a balm that can begin to heal our unresolved sin so that we never want to put on a mask again. Those who receive this gift live in profound and sacred health . . . without fail . . . always.

Degenerated Love

You may be surprised to learn that this gift of love is not about "learning to love more" or "learning to love better." In God's world, receiving love comes *before* giving love. We learn how to love only when we first learn how to receive the love of God and others. "We love because he first loved us."[1]

We so much want to *do* something. Most of us have never been taught how to let something *be* done to us. We haven't learned the fine art of *receiving love*. But because we've been urged to love others, we charge forth to inflict others with our "love."

Our friend, Don, turned love into a hurtful imitation of the real thing. He is a quick-thinking, fast-acting investment broker whose family of origin probably invented the word *dysfunction*. As we were mentoring Don on learning to receive love, he told us: "All my Christian life I was challenged to love other people. But why? Why would anyone want my version of love? That's just asking for trouble. These were *my* love gifts: arrogance packaged as teaching; control disguised as protection; manipulation wrapped as concern; exploitation marketed as opportunities. How 'bout them love gifts! Until I learned how to *be* loved, my 'loving' just spewed all my junk and debris onto others."

A Process of Meeting Needs

The knowledge that we are loved will never peel away our masks or heal our wounds. "Knowing about love" and "experiencing love" are not the same thing.[2] They come from two different planets . . . or two different rooms. In The Room of Good Intentions we will hear a lot about love, and our spirituality may even be assessed by how much we "love" (do for) others. However, in The Room of Grace we actually learn to *receive* the gift of love—to experience it.

When we are ready to receive love, we will know, because we will begin to *experience a process* with the following steps:

1. I understand that I have needs.
2. I realize that having my needs met is experiencing love.
3. I freely admit that I desire to be loved.
4. I choose to let you love me.
5. I let you love me—on your terms, not mine.
6. I am fulfilled when I have experienced love.
7. I am now able to love others out of my own fulfillment.

STEP ONE: I Understand That I Have Needs

In our coaching forums we occasionally ask people to get away by themselves for a while and list their *needs* for developing spiritual health and maturity. A need is something required and indispensable—a must. A number of people come back with a very short list, some with a completely blank page. Some don't come back at all. They just *need* a nap!

What causes us to overlook or avoid the basic requirements for our health and maturity—our needs? The principal reason is that we see our needs as weaknesses. Ironically, we have no problem accepting our need to breathe as imperative for our physical health. Meeting our need for security, attention, and acceptance is just as normal and necessary for our spiritual health as meeting our need for oxygen is for our physical health. Sin influences people to define their innate needs as weaknesses. "I don't need you" is the language of the wounded heart.

Our weaknesses are actually those attitudes and behaviors that emerge because of the unresolved sin in us. Our weaknesses also stem from our unwillingness to accept our limitations. For example, if I'm not athletic enough to dunk a basketball, then I lie about a knee injury.

If we see needs as weaknesses, we will hide our needs and limitations and call it self-reliance. Or we'll pretend that we have no needs and call it independence. Or we may believe no one should ever have to meet our needs and call it strength. Or we believe that as we get more "spiritual," we outgrow our needs. This, we say, is maturity.

Some of us take our aversion to needs a step beyond weaknesses — we actually confuse our needs with sin. That must thrill God. He's the one who created needs. Needs do not come from sin, and they are not sin. Adam and Eve needed the love of God long before they sinned! God communicated with them and fulfilled their needs in that relationship of love. God accepted them. He gave them security. He gave them attention and boundaries for their health and safety.[3] Needs are not sin, but sin has distorted our understanding of needs. In our destructive, self-centered world, we hardly know what to do with our needs.

So, the first step in receiving the gift of love is to understand that we have needs. Once we believe that, we are ready for step two.

STEP TWO: I Realize That Having My Needs Met Is Experiencing Love

Why did God create us with needs? Most of us have never thought about this before: Without needs we cannot experience love — we cannot know when we are being loved.

Think about it. A desk has no need to be loved. We may say we "love" a certain desk, but disappointing as it may be to some, the desk will never know our love. It has no capacity for love. Needs give us the capacity to feel loved. We know or experience love when our needs are met. This is why we say that love is the process of meeting needs.

Every day we need to be loved. Every day our God is committed to meeting our needs for attention—his servant love[4]; acceptance—God's unearned love[5]; security—God's committed love[6]; trust—God's faithful love[7]; guidance—his disciplined love[8]; truth—God's instructional love[9]; protection—God's jealous love[10]; significance—God's affirming love[11]; and so forth. These needs never go away.

Sadly, if we cannot identify our needs, we cannot know love. If we deny we have needs, we will not experience love. If we withhold our needs, we can't receive the love others have for us. And, if we don't know love, we'll be stuck with open wounds that will not heal—those nasty Inevitable Effects. And, when our needs go unmet, we are truly unhappy people. Period.

STEP THREE: I Freely Admit That I Desire to Be Loved

Deep within each of us resides the desire to be loved. Oh, but the pain and risk of love! We creatively fashioned some of the oldest masks in our closet to make others think that, at least in our case, love is optional. These masks come complete with habitual mannerisms, clever responses, and insulating possessions all ingenuously designed to convince others that we have no longing to be loved.

Into our silliness God often steps in and arranges circumstances to expose our absurd antics. He graciously turns our denial into a life-changing admission that, "Boy-howdy, how I desire to be loved!" Such a God-moment happened to Rick, one of Bill's students in a graduate class. Rick heatedly interrupted Bill's teaching to declare that he had no needs. Rick explained that now that he had his relationship with the Lord, the Word of God, and his responsibility as a Bible teacher, all his significant needs had been met. He was adamant and became the focus of attention in that class.

The following week Rick stood up in class and asked if he could explain what had happened to him the previous week in a church class he was teaching. He then proceeded to tell the class that shortly after he began teaching, a gentleman named Joe sat down in the front row and started weeping. Rick was deeply disconcerted because there had never been much emoting during his teaching before. He kept on teaching, but Joe wept through the entire class. After the session everyone left the room, except Joe. He walked up to Rick and said, "I really need you to help me." Joe was now sobbing loudly. Rick replied, "Well, I'm not a counselor, but maybe I can listen to your problem." Joe explained that he was devastated because two days earlier his wife of more than fifteen years left him for another man and moved away overnight. Rick was deeply affected by this man's words but didn't know how to show it. He eventually gave Joe a clumsy hug, trying to care for him.

At this point, Rick slowly looked around Bill's classroom and told everyone that some years earlier his wife had also walked out on *him*. He had not told this to anyone at the school before. He had tears in his eyes. Then he looked at Bill and said, "I was wrong. I have incredible needs and I have frozen them all these years. I have lived in denial. I so wanted what you were teaching not to be true because I never wanted to be hurt again. Last week, when I stood up, I was projecting onto everyone else a denial of my pain. I was filled with resentment for what my wife had done to me. For me to admit that I had needs meant I had to risk being loved again. I know God sent Joe to remind me of the pain. I have lived in isolation from love all these years." He then wept openly and told the class, "I am unbelievably miserable and I need help."

Thousands know Rick's pain. The loss of his wife devastated him, and he thought he had figured out a way to deal with it: I will take care of myself. I won't get that close again. Just like so many others, he assumed his needs for intimacy, acceptance, security, affirmation, and the like would go away. But God hardwired needs into us—they don't go away.

Rick hid his pain somewhere deep within so it wouldn't embarrass him anymore. Little did he know that this choice of denying his Involuntary Response of hurt would cause him to experience the Inevitable Effects of shame, blame, fear, denial, and anger. Rick had not recognized the devastating sequence of unresolved sin. But you can. If God speaks to you through Rick's story, it means he may not need to send you a "man in the front row" before you freely admit that you want to be loved.

Many of us have spent years perfecting our self-protection routines. We have carefully, stone by stone, erected a drafty castle that we thought would safeguard us from the pain of broken relationships. Some of us had "good reasons" to erect that castle. But we now know that these walls have never truly protected us—they have just kept us isolated and alone. Our only companions were those nasty gangsters, the Inevitable Effects of shame, blame, fear, denial, and anger.

Our castle walls won't come down just because someone says they should. They start coming down when we admit:

- Step one, we have needs;
- Step two, we can only experience love when our needs are met; and
- Step three, we really, really want to be loved.

And, that, our friends, is when the fun begins!

STEPS FOUR & FIVE: I Choose to Let You Love Me — on Your Terms, Not Mine

After chronicling Sharon's shocking childhood in chapter 1, we wrote that she'd be back to tell "the rest of the story." We tell that story here to give you hope. Rarely has any child been subjected to such ongoing treachery and evil as Sharon, and yet today all three of us consider her one of the healthiest and most mature leaders in our lives. If God can resolve her sin and the sin done against her, he can do it for you too. How did Sharon progress from such devastation to mature influence? Much of it occurred right here through steps four and five.

As an adult, Sharon invested years designing and building one of the more exquisite self-protection structures around. She says, "I built the Great Wall of China." But, behind this formidable wall, those relentless Inevitable Effects ultimately wore her out. When she could take no more, Sharon started asking questions, and a friend began walking with her down the trail of Trusting God. Sharon admitted her needs and that they would never be met unless she learned to receive love. In time, she began trusting who God says she is, and that ushered her right into The Room of Grace.

Not long after that, Sharon began realizing the central role trust would continue to play in her healing and maturity. She learned the fundamental truth behind step four: <u>The degree to which I let you love me is the degree to which you can love me, no matter how much love you have for me.</u> That wouldn't have been a problem for Sharon, except the "let" requires trust! We cannot let another person love us unless we trust the person.[12]

People who are unable to trust will never experience love. Ever. One can't find a way through that particular cul-de-sac. Despite the years of abuse, Sharon avoided that lonely life, because she learned to entrust herself to God and others. If anyone had reason never to trust again, it was Sharon. But she let people love her and her needs began to be met in a profound way. Grace, when it is conceived in trust, begets astonishing resolution, healing, maturity, and powerful influence.

Many people who deeply want to be loved are not loved, because they won't turn that doorknob of Humility—"trusting God and others with me." They stand out in the cold, outside The Room of Grace, in pain (and blame) because people don't love them. But Sharon's life demonstrates this truth: The people God wants to use to love you deeply and to meet your needs stand right on the other side of that door. Turn the knob.

There's another dimension of receiving love that Sharon's story illustrates. Step five says, "I let you love me on your terms, not mine." When Sharon was first learning to receive love, she demanded that people do this or buy that or serve her in the way she deemed best. But, as she matured in receiving love, she realized that submitting to others to meet her needs required that she let them discern how to address her needs. In learning to receive love, we cannot forget that others are the ones with the strengths that can meet our needs. We are the ones with both the needs and the inability to meet them. Learning to let others love us on their terms is part of what it means to "submit to one another out of reverence for Christ."[13]

If, despite our need for acceptance and people's moves to include us, we continually reject them because we want them to meet our needs on our terms, we will remain unloved and in the darkness of our unresolved sin. We cannot experience another's acceptance, love, or guidance unless we let that person give us these things.

> Lost in the darkness
> Silence surrounds you.
> Once there was morning
> Now endless night.
>
> If I could reach you,
> I'd guide you and teach you
> To walk from the darkness
> Back to the Light.[14]

Will others meet our needs perfectly and will we trust perfectly? No. This is The Room of Grace, remember? "Grace is the face love wears, when it meets imperfection." Learning to love perfectly or trust perfectly is not the point; rather, it's learning to receive love. We can't wait for perfect people before we trust people. That's like standing in line at the DMV without a number and expecting prompt service. It ain't gonna happen!

Further, when we on the basis of trust receive God's perfect love for us, it pushes away our fear and teaches us to embrace the love that heals our wounds.[15] In The Room of Good Intentions, where self-protection rules, we put everything in jeopardy—our healing, our maturing, and our reason for being on this earth. But in The Room of Grace we have learned that God won't let us down, even when others do. When they turn away, we remember he won't.[16] He's our safety net. He's got our back. Trusting God frees us to move into these relationships. Trusting God frees our hearts to experience his safe, constant, intimate sufficiency. Sharon would tell you that this solid strength of trusting God—who can't let us down—allows us to move toward others in love despite the risk. And that propels us into a different dimension of living.

STEP SIX: I Am Fulfilled When I Have Experienced Love

Trusting God is the path that leads us into The Room of Grace where we gradually receive the supreme gift of grace—love. If we have spent our lives building walls of self-protection, it will take time and trust for us to unwrap this gift. But when we receive love—when we are loved—we feel fulfilled. Love completely satisfies our longings, ambitions, and potential. God, the ultimate fulfiller, invites us to trust him. Those who hang out very long in The Room of Grace always experience too much love to return to a life without such a gift.

What does this new way of living do to a person? For those who've never or rarely experienced it before, it is nothing short of miraculous. Others can actually see a real and lasting difference. Wives look at their husbands, shake their heads, and ask, "Who are you, and where has my husband gone?" Received love turns frightened pretenders into confident dreamers. It even turns violent lions into humble and tender receivers of love.

Maybe pain is the reason you are reading this book. You know something is wrong and don't know how to fix it. Maybe you know you are hurting others and don't know how to stop. Maybe your pain is the absence of peace. Maybe your pain is the worst type of all—the pain of hiding, isolated in a private world where love cannot penetrate.

Centuries ago, as legend has it, an escaped slave named Androcles fled into a forest where he wandered upon a loudly growling lion. Androcles started to run, but when he noticed that the lion did not pursue him, he turned around and slowly approached it. At that point the lion lifted out its paw, swollen and bleeding. Androcles immediately saw the source of the pain—a huge thorn had buried itself deep within the lion's paw. With great courage, knowing that the removal of the thorn would temporarily increase the lion's pain and possibly incite it to attack, Androcles removed the thorn and bound up the paw. When he finished, the lion licked Androcles' hand like a dog and took the young man to its cave. Every day the lion would bring meat to him.

Then, one day, both Androcles and the lion were captured. Their captors decided to withhold food from the lion for several days, and when it was good and hungry, they would throw Androcles to the lion to be eaten. When the appointed day arrived, the emperor and his court came to witness the spectacle. Androcles was led into the middle of the arena and the lion was loosed from its cage. Immediately the lion roared at its victim—but then recognized a friend. The lion stopped and leaned into Androcles, rubbed its face against the young man's, and then licked his hand again, like a dog. Shocked, the emperor summoned Androcles, who recounted the entire story. The emperor set Androcles free and returned the lion to its home in the forest.

As beautiful as this fable is, it is not even close to the beauty we can find when we allow others to love us. Andrea, our close friend, was not unlike the lion. Brilliant, well-read, shrewd, and intimidatingly competent, Andrea always made you feel like back-pedaling in her presence. John says, "I always felt if I were to make a mistake or say something uninformed in her presence, I'd be instantly and forever labeled, and then banished by her into the huddled masses of the dim-witted. I'd politely try to answer her questions, sounding more like a politician behind in the polls than myself. She was strong, sharp-tongued, blunt, and overwhelming."

We had no way of knowing that Andrea's paw had been swollen and bleeding for some time. She was simply trying to find out, in her own way, if we would answer her gruffness in kind, or if we could help pull out her thorn. We provided Andrea with an environment of acceptance, affirmation, protection, and truth, and this environment helped her feel safe. Along with others in our community, we saw Andrea as a saint—a saint with claws, to be sure, but still a saint! Yes, sometimes her claws hurt us, but that's what happens when we live in The Room of Grace. Grace-givers understand this. After all, Jesus, who was full of grace and truth, took all of our pain on himself so that we could be healed.[17]

For several months, Andrea's pain drove her to seek out several of us to whom she could bare her heart's pain. Her world wasn't working. Her mask-of-choice caused her to feel lonely and unloved. She could not receive the love we offered her. But this lioness had the courage to humble her heart and dared to trust some fallible and fragile people to do what she could not do for herself—meet her deep need for security, for dependency, for hope. At first, Andrea's requests for help were clumsy. After all, this was unfamiliar territory for her. But it made her story all the more lovely to those of us who knew and loved her.

Because of her humble choice to receive love, Andrea now lets others love her. It is hard to believe she is the same woman! Losing none of her competency, she has become a lover of others and a playful friend who laughs often and cries freely. We feel safe around her and have known her continual affirmation and trust.

Andrea is a powerful woman who travels in powerful circles. But if we are ever pitted against each other in the arena, we know Andrea will look into our eyes, lean into us, and rub her face against ours—no matter how great the pressure or how hungry she is in the pain of what sin has done against her. Andrea is fulfilled in love, and now she has enough for others, which leads us to the final step.

STEP SEVEN: I Am Now Able to Love Others Out of My Own Fulfillment

Having our needs met by receiving the love of God and others is not just about "feeling better"; it's about fulfillment. To *fulfill* means "to meet the requirements of, to satisfy."[18] When the requirements of our soul—our needs—are met, it satisfies us. This fulfillment produces inward peace, contentment, and healing for our wounds. As our wounds heal, we can turn away from them with a fresh passion, confidence, and love for others. To serve others out of a contented, fulfilled soul is like rubbing eucalyptus oil onto the sore muscles of a friend. The person gets healing and the whole room smells wonderful.

Millions of people have yet to meet the King of Love. When they see us living in blame, shame, fear, denial, and anger, with no real answers, it confuses them. When they see us attempting to mask those dysfunctions, it tells them not to trust us—or the God we follow. When they see us focused on wounds that never heal, they conclude we cannot deal with theirs. That's a major reason why life in The Room of Good Intentions is such a waste. It never produces an environment conducive to people courageously attempting their first footsteps of trusting the grace and love of Jesus Christ.

If it is unerringly true that each of us enjoys only the love we will allow in, and if it is equally true that God went to unending lengths to bring us love in a way that we would allow in, then it becomes stunningly obvious that the carriers of God's love ought to be wildly driven to learn to give his love in a way that can be easily put on.

To give a love that can be trusted changes everything. This is where life gets worth living. It jump-starts one of the most profoundly beautiful and miraculous chain reactions we get to witness in this lifetime. Closed, broken, frightened, bluffing men and women come squinting out of the dark corners into the light and start singing songs they didn't know were in them. They begin to feel alive—secure in his embrace, seeing life for the first time in full color. Actually allowing this love past their double-bolted defenses, they wonder out loud what took them so long. Each one becomes real, safe, creative, and refreshingly untamed. They drink this love in like those gulping down cold, fresh lemonade for the first time. And they almost involuntarily begin to offer to all around them a love as rich and freeing as what they are taking in. They discover a waiting, thirsty community everywhere they look. And the world around them dramatically changes, one drink at a time . . .

≡ DID YOU DISCOVER?

- Love, the first gift of grace, acts as a solvent to lift our masks off our faces.

- Those who receive this gift live in profound and sacred health . . . without fail.

- In God's world, receiving love comes *before* giving love.

- When we are ready to receive love, we will know, because we will begin to *experience a process* with the following steps:

  - I understand that I have needs.

  - I realize that having my needs met *is* experiencing love.

  - I freely admit that I desire to be loved.

  - I choose to let you love me.

  - I let you love me; on your terms, not mine.

  - I am fulfilled when I have experienced love.

  - I am now able to love others out of my own fulfillment.

- "I don't need you" is the language of the wounded heart.

- Needs give us the capacity to be loved and to feel loved.

- The degree to which I *let* you love me is the degree to which you *can* love me, no matter how much love you have for me.

- Trusting God's perfect love for us pushes away our fear and teaches us to embrace the love that heals our wounds.

- Love completely satisfies our longings, ambitions, and potential.

- When the requirements of our souls—our needs—are met, it satisfies us.

CHAPTER FIVE

The Sweetest Gift of Grace: Repentance

Many have the space of repentance, who have not the grace of repentance.
—William Secker

$\equiv$**F**ew of us would call repentance the "sweetest gift." For most of us repentance has been neither a gift nor sweet. A more fit analogy, in our minds, would be to compare repentance to a bitter-tasting cough syrup. We know we need to take it to cure our cough, but we hate it. It tastes like liquid linoleum! So we avoid it as long as possible, in hopes that our cough will simply heal itself. When it gets worse, and only as a last resort, we force it down.

When we don't know how to deal with our sin, we will try to hide it. That's why The Room of Good Intentions turns into such a masquerade ball. It's dress-up time! We know what we've done . . . we know what we *do*. And no amount of sadness, striving, or penance has done anything but compound our sadness. What we really need is a way home. We've been told to confess our sin, but we don't like that answer. We want to do something! Besides, we've confessed our sin a thousand times before, and what good did it do?

But when we walk around with unresolved sin, it's as if we're wearing a heavily insulated parka on the hottest day of the summer . . . in the Sahara! We're suffocating and can't figure out why. Repentance is the zipper out of that parka.

In the middle of our misery, Jesus taps us on the shoulder and says, "I have something for you that cost me everything to get for you. Here, it's a gift of my grace for you." Written across the gift is one word: repentance. The attached card reads: "Take it, apply it, and trust me to make it real. I love you. Jesus."

Some may question, "How can repentance be a gift if I am the one who's doing the repenting?" It is a gift of God's grace because your repentance literally doesn't have a chance without grace. Grace alone resolves sin. Grace alone heals, and grace alone gives power over sin. Only the power of the Cross can break a pattern of sinful behavior. That's what makes repentance a gift that only Jesus can give. No one else died to bring us such power.

Willpower Is No Power

Yet many of us act as if repentance is a matter of the will. It's not. We cannot make a decision to stop sinning. We can't "will" ourselves into change. We can't "will" ourselves into feeling contrition or remorse. Repentance isn't doing something about our sin; rather, it means admitting that we *can't* do anything about our sin. We cannot woo ourselves into anything but the most external form of repentance.

All of our effort, striving, and willpower have only momentary, external value when it comes to fighting an opponent as crafty, intentional, persistent, powerful, and experienced as sin. To confirm this, we only have to look at all the legalistic Judaizers and Pharisees who've ever walked this earth. They believe they are godly because they have the willpower to deal with certain sin-related behaviors. Yet Jesus condemns them for trusting in themselves and having contempt for others.[1]

Understand this: The *intention* not to sin is not the same as the *power* not to sin. God did not design us to conquer sin on our own. To think we can is an incalculable *under*valuing of sin's power combined with a huge overvaluing of our own willpower!

A Classic Oxymoron: Sin Management

Unfortunately, some of us fool ourselves into believing we can manage our sin, because we can stop from doing some things. Sometimes we learn to pick up our clothes after multiple reprimands . . . or we stop drinking diet soda after friends and relatives keep warning us of the ingredients . . . or we start driving the speed limit after our fifth speeding ticket. We think that because our will was sufficient enough to change some habits, we can tackle the big dog of sin.

Sin cannot be managed. If we make this our goal in repentance, we are doomed to fail. Think back to what we've said about motives, values, and actions. Our goal isn't to solve all of our sin issues. Our motive is to trust God so we can live out of who God says we are . . . so that *together* we can work on our sin issues. When we try to manage our sin through willpower, the process looks something like this:

> Sin . . . confess . . . do better for a while, then sin again. Embarrassment, confess again, ask God to take away the desire, then sin again, confess again, sin again, confess again, shock, more determination to stop sinning, think about it a lot, examine it. Make promises, create some boundaries, and sin again, now even worse than before. Despair, anger, shame, distance from God, guilt. Self-condemnation, self-loathing . . . sin again. Disillusionment, doubt, self-pity, resentment at God: *Why doesn't he hear my prayers? Why doesn't he do something?* More anger. Then fear that we allow ourselves to get angry with God. Then real confession, a heartfelt

one, and a sense of cleansing. Ah, a new start. Things seem better. *Yeah, I've finally got this sin under control.* Oops, sin again. Desperate efforts, bargains struck. Once-and-for-all healing. Really mean it this time. Sin again. Lose hope, give up, rationalize, minimize, blame, pull away, hide, judge others, put on a mask, go past the sin again, and so on.

This scenario, in varying degrees, depicts the pattern many Christians live out all their lives. This roller coaster ride has no happy ending. It only causes us to feel beaten down, to compromise our integrity, to feel cynical about this second-class life we lead.

Worse, a sin-management system shuts off the *only resource* that can deal with sin: our *trust* in who God says we are, attracting the *power* of his *grace*.

Confession Is Limited

Confession does not resolve our sin either. To be sure, admitting our sin is an important part of the process—but words do not resolve sin. We can be sorry for something we have done wrong, and even confess it, and still desire to continue doing it. Agreeing that we have done something wrong is not the same as trusting God with what we have done. Confession is not the same as truly needing God to free us of the sin we have done. Sin is resolved when we are cleansed of it, and only dependence upon the Cross of Jesus cleanses us from sin.[2] There is power there.

How does grace make repentance a gift for us—a gift that actually resolves our sin issues?

Grace-Empowered Repentance

When grace introduces us to repentance, the two of us become best friends. When anything else introduces us to repentance, it feels like the warden has come to lock us up. But when grace gets involved, the truths of repentance reveal a fabulous world of life-freeing beauty. What, then, are the truths of repentance that grace produces?

First, repentance is about trusting, not willing. Yes, there is choice involved, but if our *motive* is determined straining to please God, all our striving will be a pile of filthy rags.[3] We can do nothing—absolutely nothing to make provision for our sin. In repentance we depend on God to turn water into wine. Trust in our act of repentance releases the gift of God's grace to transform our hope into reality.

What does trust attract? Grace, in the form of power, which comes to us *directly* from God's Spirit and then *indirectly* through others. A striver cannot access this power. We cannot quantify this power, but we can measure it—in the people who actually turn away from their previous path of destruction.

Remember, trusting God with ourselves allows us to receive love—his love and the love of others. And because we're loved, we can face what we have done to others and ourselves without having to retreat to a cave of hiddenness. Love acts as a safety net that can keep us from destruction as we admit the truth about ourselves. We know that nothing we do can change how God sees us. We also realize that there are people who will not change their assessment of our worth or the commitment of their love. Grasping that single truth makes us alive with creativity and risk, safe in the strong arms of real acceptance. We stop looking over our shoulder, waiting for that shoe we always feared was about to drop. Love catches the shoe on its way down . . . every time.

When we feel safe, we are much more disposed to open our hearts to God. When we feel safe, we let go of our self-defense and call out to him, saying, "God, I no longer have anything to prove. I have nothing to hold on to. I want only what you want for me." At that instant, we know we did not create such a response. God, in his grace, gave it to us when we chose to trust him. He graced our hearts; he gave the power; he will give the strength.

Many, many Christians do not trust God in the process of repentance. They view repentance as something they *should* do, but this preempts the power. Perhaps they have been taught that when they sin, they need only confess it, to agree it's wrong. But what's missing is the hope of it being defeated.

Every act of repentance depends on an act of redemption. *To redeem* means "to liberate by payment or to release from debt or blame."[4] Willpower, no matter how sincere, cannot buy you this freedom. There is no dealing with any sin without a redemptive act.

Bill was thirty years old and had been a Christian for thirteen years when he learned what a powerful gift repentance can be. Nobody needed to tell him that he had sin issues in his life, but one night he saw the devastating effect of what that sin was doing to him and those he loved. He had just lost his job, his reputation was damaged, and he was in the worst financial trouble of his life. Yet his internal life was even worse:

> I struggled with pornography. I compromised my integrity because I wanted to look good instead of telling the truth. I blamed others for what happened to my career. It was their fault we didn't have enough money. I knew a lot of it had to do with some bad choices on my part, and yet I couldn't admit that, in my deep insecurity.

Bill didn't understand how to be relieved of those sins. Looking back, he can see that his honest confession to his wife, Grace, three years earlier had opened a door for the Holy Spirit to sharpen his awareness for his need to repent of what was true about him. Grace's love offered Bill a place of safety and acceptance that invited him to trust even more.

Even though he had been a Christian for years, Bill had never realized it was possible that every sin he committed and every sin that had been done to him could be redeemed and healed. And, he didn't know what repentance had to do with it. The truth that Bill kept hearing on this night was, "As you have received the Lord Jesus Christ, so walk in him."[5] Bill faced the life-changing reality that there is no difference between the power to save and the power to resolve sin. Jesus could release him from the power of the sin that had such an immense hold on his life. By God's grace, he did and he does. God was healing Bill then, when he received Christ, and he is healing him now. But healing requires Bill to face God with what is true about him and to trust God to cleanse him. Bill had brought his sin to the Lord many, many times before. What was different about that night?

> I stopped walking down that road of self-effort. I realized that confessing had only brought temporary relief. That night I walked off the well-worn path of Pleasing God and started walking down the road of Trusting God. Childlike trust pleases God most.

When we repent through trust, it is exclusively and entirely a gift of God's grace. That's where the power is. This kind of repentance actually provides a real power over sin. The work of Jesus is for every sin, not just for the forgiveness of that sin, but for the healing from that sin.[6]

What Inhibits Repentance?

So why is it that we can say, "This time, God, I really mean it" and yet not see resolution for our sin? By now you know that people in The Room of Good Intentions hold radically different assumptions about how to handle sin than those in The Room of Grace. The environment of the first room actually inhibits repentance, while the second one releases it. Notice three specific inhibitors of repentance.

Isolation. In The Room of Good Intentions, we don't want others to know about our sin. We want to keep our sin private, between God and us. Many times we begin to trust our own assessment of how we are doing with God. In our private thoughts, we establish our own benchmarks for godliness.

When our "repentance" functions in isolation rather than in community, it almost always indicates that we remain more concerned about personal appearances than the resolution of sin. We don't want people to think we are ungodly—to think less of us. The fact that our sin remains hidden from others proves we still favor presenting a nicely packaged life to others, while keeping sin quasi-managed and submerged. Yet genuine repentance desires to resolve *anything* and *everything* about our sin. No cover, no posturing, just pure repentance. God built that desire into the gift.[7]

Pride. When our environment values striving to please God, we won't welcome repentance as a gift. Why? We've too much to prove to God, others, and ourselves. If we publicly repent, others will know that we have not done very well in our striving. That would be like getting a C– in godliness. Better to spin the truth a bit and tell others we are doing well. Better yet, point out ways in which others have messed up. That takes the focus off of us, moving us precariously close to the precipice of an unrepentant spirit. Pride—trust in ourselves—edges out repentance. Then, as Henry and Richard Blackaby write, "Pride will do what sin does. It destroys."[8]

Wrong Motive. In the event that we attempt repentance in The Room of Good Intentions, it will be out of a motive to make God happy with us, to become more godly. When we speak bold words of determined striving to please God, those words do not spring out of a motive of Trusting God. It is so easy to relapse into that willpower kick. It's us trying to impress God again, without his grace. But trying to repent without grace is like trying to swim without water.

Resolute striving to *please* God begets a pride that keeps us focused on our own "power"—which is not a power to write home about. In contrast, repentance that comes from God is outfitted with otherworldly power—potency secured by Jesus' death and activated by his resurrection. Repentance is formidable against sin only because of actual power—the power of the Cross. Our words or religious techniques have nothing to do with it. The power in this gift reminds us of the power in the ark of the covenant, a power so mighty that the Hebrews dared not come in contact with it.[9] The same power that resided in the ark is the power in this gift. But now, God invites us to come near his grace-wrapped power.

When we receive this sweet gift of repentance, a force is unleashed that can transform our hardened, contemptuous, alienated hearts into the most tender, loving, and gentle of souls. The word *sweet* has synonyms like "gratifying," "satisfying," and "fulfilling." They aptly define repentance. How sweet it is![10]

The Mindset of a Grace-Filled Community

By now, we understand why the community of good intentions experiences far less repentance than the community of grace. When we venture in that direction, we will do so without the grace needed to resolve our sin. Yet, in a grace-filled community, a different view of life in God biases the whole culture toward repentance. For starters, this community expects and anticipates imperfection. Yes, we honor others in the community as saints, but we also face the reality of each other's sin. We applaud vulnerability and view godliness as something much more than the presence of good behavior and the absence of bad behavior. We're too busy dancing to hold on to that dead weight. The individuals in this community trust God to mature them from the inside out, by the power of his Spirit . . . in his timing. No one feels a need to hide, for no one's parading his or her own righteousness. Everyone feels safe to be real and alive.

In such a community, repentance is as accessible to its members as fast food is to city dwellers. This community keeps repentance handy in the cupboard, ready to draw on its grace-power at a moment's notice. This group wouldn't go to bed at night without embracing repentance to ensure ongoing healing and love. It's a community of saints, after all. Saints who sin.

Picture this. Into the community of grace comes a hurting, tired, broken-down saint who has spent all her Christian life in a community of folks with good intentions. She's plowed through a number of relationships and hurt a lot of people on the way to this door. Now she has stumbled into an environment filled with people for whom trusting God in repentance is a way of life.

What difference will this community make in her life? A mask-shattering difference—a miraculous, life-changing reformation. These folk treat her for who she is: a saint. They deal with her sin the way God deals with theirs: by standing with her, with their arms around her. They commit to loving her, and they begin to show her how to receive their love. They accept her. They choose to see her like Jesus does. They let her into their own lives.

So far, so good. But what happens when one day she confesses, "I have lied. I have hurt those closest to me. I have betrayed my husband.

I've deceived all of you too." Oops. What does the community do now? Do they cower from her? Tell her that what she did isn't that bad, that she'll get over it? Convince her she was probably right? Do they give her nonverbal signals that they don't approve of such revelations? No. After maybe one or more share their own story of failure, they tell her a new story about this beautiful gift used quite routinely in the community. Then they ask her, "Do you remember how you've learned to receive love? You trusted God and others for it. Well, my friend, that's how you get this gift too. Just lean into God. Depend on what he tells you and trust his lead."

Don't you think this woman might actually try trusting God for his gift of repentance? In such environments repentance becomes a way of life. And when that happens, grace heals, matures, reconciles, and unleashes the love of God through people. And the community of broken healers becomes more beautiful by the day. One day this woman stands near the door, waiting for the next wounded soul to stumble in, so she can be one of the first to tell the new story of this gift . . . a gift "used quite routinely in the community."

When failing strivers stumble into a community of grace, safety, and vulnerable repentance, it radically disrupts their game plan. Suddenly, they are face to face with a real, tangible option of sweet freedom. And the ongoing environment of the community tells them that they have not dreamed up this way of life. As the community treats them as they have never been treated before, their confidence grows that grace can support the full weight of their sin.

Repentance Will Set You Free

During his late teens, Bruce battled the dark-heartedness of "guilt trips" when he didn't live up to either his own or others' expectations of him. He wanted so much to prove himself to God and others. Drivenness would kick in during these seasons and, not surprisingly, his behavior hurt others and himself. Bruce says, "About that time, I could've really used a spiritual director like the one who told Brennan Manning, 'Brennan, give up trying to look good and sound like a saint. It will be a lot easier on everybody.'"[11] Even though Bruce tried his hardest, he could not break loose of this pattern. He wore out many pairs of shoes on the try-harder path of Pleasing God. Strange how directions get confused—God didn't even want Bruce on that dangerous stretch of road, and Bruce was never quite convinced that his sold-out efforts of moral striving to make God happy and impress others were working. He grew exhausted struggling to overcome this pattern, while at the same time, devaluing the wounds he caused others.

During these months, deepening pain eventually prompted Bruce to self-reflection on power—the power of grace versus what he brought to the table. That season eventually freed Bruce into a powerful repentance that broke the old cycle and began a whole new life pattern. His words went something like this:

> All right, God, I cannot conquer this recurring sin. And it
> is hurting people. I will not build my life around creating
> a security for myself that you've already secured. I trust
> your conclusion about me, not my own. Lord Jesus, I
> lean into your power for breaking this cycle.

"Leaning into" (trusting) these truths applied the power of the Cross directly to Bruce's previously unbreakable pattern. Has Bruce ever relapsed onto the Pleasing God road? Oh, for sure. He knows that trail by heart. But, the Cross—not Bruce's prayer, not his confession— powered a whole new way of living for Bruce. It is infinitely more relaxing, more freeing, and more maturing. He will not go back to that way of life.

When grace brings truth to light, it sometimes does so through love (as we learned in the last chapter), sometimes through forgiveness (as we'll learn in the next chapter), and sometimes through repentance. The principles of God's grace play off of each other. Grace begets repentance, and repentance nurtures forgiveness. Trust attracts grace, and grace helps saints to trust. Even goofed-up, compromised, failed, and confused saints. *Especially* them.

When repentance becomes a constant, recognizable part in an environment, the people in that culture experience freedom they never knew. They have amazing stories to tell. The truth always sets us free. Free to love God and others, free to trust even more truth, free to heal and reconcile, free to bring reconciliation to those who still don't know the Reconciler, free to follow our callings and dreams.

Learning to Trust Like We Did the First Time

Do we really trust God? Even more specifically, do we really believe the God we trust is strong enough and powerful enough to heal us? That is the bottom line. It may be easier to believe that Jesus died for all our sin so that we can go to heaven, somewhere out there in the distant future. But the power to heal habitual, present sin? Sin that's here and now; that's noisy, agonizing, hot, angry, and very, very real? We typically reason, *I think God will get me to heaven, but I'm really not sure he can handle this one.*

So, trusting God for his grace in repentance prompts us to ask:

- "God, are you strong enough to heal my patterns of self-destruction?"
- "God, do you always have my best interests at heart?"
- "God, are you able to take care of me if I live without the mask, if I walk around with no devices for self-protection?"
- "God, are you able to vindicate me if I do not vindicate myself?"

- "God, are you able to deal with my sin if I make the decision to turn away from my willpower and turn toward trusting in your power?"
- "God, are you able to protect me when in disclosure I am vulnerable to others knowing what is true about me?"

As we exercise our trust, we receive his grace. Just like we did the first time we met him.

Repentance at Any Age

John's daughter Amy is bright and alive and fun and beautiful. She is also stubborn and prone to her father's obsessive tendencies. Not too long ago, Amy broke the heart of a neat young man by allowing their relationship to move too quickly. At times Amy has been in love with the thought of being in love. After her emotions cool, she backs away to "just be friends." She did this with this particular young man, and it hurt him. We'll let John tell the story:

> I don't think I would've been bothered as a father so much except that I really liked this guy. He really liked her. And this was not her first time hurting a boy she liked. Amy had walked through this process twice before.
>
> So, one morning I took her out for breakfast at our neighborhood International House of Pancakes. I bumbled my way into sharing my concern about her relationships. She got defensive and aloof. She said she was sorry, but she also said, "What am I supposed to do, lie to him? I don't feel more than friends with him."
>
> I was sad because she was choosing to go it alone, reacting to stuff she didn't know how to fix, not letting

anyone else in. I was sad because hurting others was hurting her and changing her. I was sad because I adore her and didn't want my daughter to live out a selfish pattern that would damage her future. I was sad because she didn't see that Jesus was hurting for her. Somewhere in the middle of mixing eggs with my hash browns, I started to cry. Amy asked me what was wrong, and I told her all those things. And I told her how sad it must make Jesus to watch her bluff through life alone, reacting and repositioning.

Something beautiful happened in that moment: Trust awakened. Tears started welling up in Amy's eyes. She said, "I don't want to live like this anymore. I don't want to hurt anyone like this anymore. I don't want to do this to one more person. I don't want to hurt Jesus. I'm sorry, Dad. I feel so sad. I don't know how to do this any better. It's like I know the right thing to do, but when I get in certain situations I change the rules and do what I think will take care of Amy in that moment. I think I've been trying to do things on my own for so long, it's all I know. But I want God to help change me. Dad, will you help me?"

I reminded her that this was the reason Jesus came—so that she'd never have to live in the shame or embarrassment of failure. I reminded her that when we come face to face with our failure, Jesus is never closer to us. I reminded her that he is not ashamed of her. I reminded her that he was deeply proud of her for being vulnerable. I reminded her that this is the basis of why we worship—God loves us more than we can love ourselves and he can solve what we cannot. I told her that she was unable to change herself simply because she was sorry. But she could put her full trust and dependency in Jesus, and he would be faithful to change her, from the inside out.

That morning my precious daughter broke the pattern of an "I'm sorry" that gets parents off her back to an "I'm sorry" that demonstrated repentance. Amy was asking for more than forgiveness. She was trusting God to help her no longer hide behind an indifference that was merely a defense for her fear of rejection. That day she experienced the sweetest gift of grace. She learned a repentance that could take off her mask and allow the process of unresolved sin to be stopped in its tracks. In that moment, my precious daughter learned not to go it alone.

When trust awakens, grace is never far away. My daughter's repentance was real. God stood with Amy, her sin in front of them, and his grace empowered her. She went to this young man, told him how sorry she was for her carelessness with his heart, and asked his forgiveness. She has maintained a real and beautiful friendship with that young man. They care for each other and protect each other and periodically write and phone each other. Amy's grace-infused repentance earned his trust. They will be friends for a long time.

In The Room of Grace no one is above anyone else. No one brags about his or her accomplishments. No one keeps score. No one is shunned. No one can lose membership for blowing it. This room is not a utopian ideal. It is a home where people live together. One of them lives under my roof. Her name is Amy.

A Prayer for You

Don't dismiss the unstoppable force of repentance, or once again you'll resort to cheesecloth and bailing wire. When you are ready to trust God's provision for resolving your sin, you will pray something like this:

> God, here we go. Here is a sin I trust you to do something about. I am convinced I cannot deal with this sin. I trust what you did at the Cross is powerful enough, not only to bring me to heaven one day, but powerful enough that it can break this very sin's power that is now plaguing my life.

≡ DID YOU DISCOVER?

- Repentance is a gift of God's grace because your repentance resolves nothing without grace. Grace alone resolves sin.

- Only the power of the Cross can break a pattern of sinful behavior.

- Repentance isn't doing something about our sin; rather, it means admitting that we *can't* do anything about our sin.

- Sin cannot be managed.

- A sin-management system shuts off the only resource that can deal with sin: our trust in who God says we are, attracting the power of his grace.

- Agreeing that we have done something wrong is not the same as trusting God with what we have done.

- We can do absolutely nothing to make provision for our sin.

- Every act of repentance depends on an act of redemption.

- Three common inhibitors of repentance are isolation, pride, and a wrong motive.

- When grace brings truth to light, it sometimes does so through love, sometimes through forgiveness, and sometimes through repentance.

CHAPTER SIX

The Most Mysterious Gift of Grace: Forgiveness

Christianity is the only religion whose God bears the scars of evil.

—Os Guinness

Forgiveness breaks down walls, frees hearts, mends countries, restores families, and draws out the best in us. It can turn hatred into tenderness and the desire to destroy into a passion to protect. It is more powerful than any weapon, government, or wealth. Nothing else can bring such profound healing. Forgiveness forms the foundation of our relationship with God and sustains our relationships with each other. When we unleash this gift, by receiving it in humble trust that God can actually free our heart and heal our relationships, then the miraculous can happen. This powerful gift has one purpose: to protect us from the insidious harm that comes from *sin done against us.*

We need a way home. We've been told to get over the sin done to us, but we can't find our way out of the shadows. We can't seem to let go of our hurt. Then, in the middle of our misery, Jesus taps us on the shoulder and says, "I have something for you that cost me everything to get for you. Here, it's a gift of my grace for you." Written across the gift is one word: forgiveness. The attached card reads: "Take it, apply it, and trust me to make it real. I love you. Jesus. "

Forgiveness produces results so far out of our normal experience that it feels mysterious. Forgiveness brings alienated enemies together again. People who hated each other. People who do whatever they can never to see or talk to each other again. People who have pledged to kill each other. People who have killed each others' family members. When people forgive, their hearts are woven together in love. This is mysterious stuff.

A Teenager's Trauma

Near the end of Bill's first semester as a high-school freshman, some of his "friends" played a devastating practical joke on him. In between classes they took off his pants in the main stairwell where kids rushed from class to class. They called it "de-pants-ing." They held Bill down long enough for dozens of people to see him naked. He especially remembered the girls walking by. The de-pants-ing didn't last long, maybe less than a minute, but the scars lasted years. When Bill finally got away from his friends, he immediately started crying and ran home. He felt incredible sadness, pain, and shame. Even today Bill can vividly remember every single moment of that minute.

Sometime during that semester Bill's family moved to Arizona. Even though he was more than two thousand miles away from those who had hurt him, he couldn't forget what they had done. Now he was angry, and his anger had an immensely profound effect. Bill began to blame that experience for why he didn't know how to get along with girls. He'd lie in bed at night plotting the deaths of his friends. He even planned how to do it so no one would ever know the culprit.

In his shame, Bill blamed his classmates for who he was becoming. His inability to resolve what they did against him led to a horrible permission. Bill began to connect many of the issues of his developing sexuality to the embarrassment of that moment.

After high school, Bill became a Christian. He went to a Bible college and learned he needed to forgive these friends. When he forgave them, God truly healed Bill of the pain of that day. That summer he also forgave his offenders face to face. We'll let him tell you about it in his own words:

> I had a house-painting business in my old hometown, and I hired three of these guys to work for me. During lunch one day, we were all sitting under a tree. I said, "You know, guys, I have something really important I want to share with you. I'd like to talk about that time you de-pantsed me."
>
> Jim quickly answered, "That was you? Gosh, that was funny! We must have laughed about that for weeks." The other two guys laughed and all of them went back to their lunch. I just sat there, stunned. This was one of the most traumatic experiences of my life and they'd forgotten to whom they'd even done it!
>
> Sin done against us profoundly affects us. Sometimes it can distort life and cause us to make some incredibly unhealthy judgments. After a while, these guys could tell that this memory was really important to me. Joe, Jim's brother, said, "Hey, I'm sorry. We were just having fun. Is there anything we can do?"
>
> Although it was awkward, I told them how that day had impacted me. I told them that my best friends should be the ones to protect me from an experience like that—they shouldn't have initiated it. I realized they'd never thought about most of what I was saying. I moved toward these guys in love and forgiveness. I needed to hear them say they were sorry, and when they told me they were, I believed they meant it, and I forgave them.

That summer Bill learned some unforgettable things about forgiveness. We'll use his story and a few others to help us understand the keys of forgiveness in their order.

KEY #1: Admit Something Happened!

God's provision for our healing always begins with our recognition that someone has sinned against us.

We often skip this first step in forgiveness for a variety of reasons. We may not realize that we have been sinned against. This is often the case when we are sinned against as a child—abused, neglected, demeaned, and so on.

Or, we may feel we will lose control of the relationship if we say we've been hurt. We think that if we don't admit it, no one will have any control over us—someone more articulate or powerful will not be able to manipulate us into believing we are the guilty party.

Or, we may want to deny that we have been hurt. We think, *This shouldn't bother me. I will just go on.* It may feel too fragile to admit we've been hurt. For example, in Bill's developing adolescence he could've determined he was just going to act tough, be macho, and say, "It was nothing. Didn't bother me at all." Fortunately, he admitted the hurt, or forgiveness would never have occurred.

We cannot forgive *until* we admit we have been sinned against. This does not mean we should start searching for all the things we haven't acknowledged were done against us. We're talking about the things we *know* have been done against us that we've chosen to deny. These offenses nag at us, and most will surface automatically. This is an invitation to stop hiding the sin that someone else has done against us. To forgive, we must admit what is already true.

KEY #2: Forgive the Consequences of the Act Done Against You

Often the consequences of the act done against us are worse—sometimes far worse—than the act of sin itself.

This was true for Bill . . . and it was true for Bruce. One of the most traumatic seasons in his life occurred when several leaders lied to him and then about him to others. He says:

> My struggle was not in forgiving these leaders for the dishonesty. I understand how false statements get made. They seem mild compared to the substantial consequences of those lies—the loss of reputation, friends, finances, and some of my dreams. These were much more heart wrenching than the lies themselves. I needed to forgive more than the dishonesty and betrayal. Only when I got in touch with the impact that the dishonesty had on my life was I able to trust God in forgiving these leaders for the specific things I held against them: the consequences of their sin against me. Without forgiving for the consequences of the lying, I could not experience healing, freedom, and reconciliation. Being freed from just the act of sin would've left me bound to the consequences.

In order to understand the effect a sin has had on us, we find it helps to write down the incident and what happened. But we can't stop there. We need to include how the incident impacted our life, to get in touch with how we felt as a result of that event. We need to ask ourselves questions like these: Did I experience shame? Did I become fearful? Did I feel demeaned and devalued? Did anger and resentment begin to grow within me? Did I feel manipulated? Was I shunned? Were there relational effects? Did I lose my marriage, my children, my friends? Did I lose a business or a sum of money? Did I lose my position or leadership role? Has this sin led to a change in my outlook or attitude toward life?

As we allow ourselves to feel the pain of our responses, we begin to understand the consequences of the sin done to us. This is critical. Harboring enables the sin that was committed against us to define us.[1] Remember, unresolved sins are buried alive, including the ones done against us. This hard work prepares us to forgive.

KEY #3: Tell God What Happened to You

Once we have acknowledged what has happened and how it affected us, we must pour out our hearts to God, telling him everything about what happened to us.

We might think he doesn't want to hear it all, but we would be wrong. We might think, *No way! This is only for emotionally based people. I don't do that stuff.* But we would be very wrong. We might think that we should be past this, and that any rehearsal of the event is akin to wallowing in it, but we would be wrong. We might think that because God already knows these things, he doesn't want to hear them again from us, but we would be wrong.

We can mumble, cry, sigh, get angry, shout, run around the room, howl like a coyote if we need to—but let's not stop short of getting in touch with all the effects and feelings inside us from that person's sin against us. We shouldn't stop until we're sure we've told God everything that happened to us. Everything.

When Bill came to the realization of the power of forgiveness, he forgave his friends for taking off his pants in the stairwell and holding him down. It took him much longer to tell God about the feelings of shame and the pain, about the multiple nights of dreaming of their demise, about his anger, about his self-consciousness, about his blaming them for the inability to date girls. But in time he got it all out. We need to do the same.

KEY #4: Forgive the Offender for Your Benefit

Forgiveness has an order—we must initiate the *vertical transaction* with God before we move into the *horizontal transaction* with others. First, before God, we forgive the offenders for what they've done and the consequences it has reaped in our life. This is between God and us, *for our sake.*[2] Then, after we've forgiven our offenders before God, we go to our offender and forgive him or her. We'll call that a *horizontal transaction.* If we don't get this right, if we move toward the person without having been cleansed before God, we risk moving toward our offender in bitterness, resentment, judgment, and a spirit of getting even. If we prematurely attempt reconciliation with the offender, we'll bring the residue of unresolved sin into the equation. And everyone can smell it. Trusting becomes harder than peddling an angry bear uphill on a unicycle.

If we try to go on without forgiving the one who hurt us before God, or if we say, "I'm not going to repent until they repent," we end up in bitterness, anger, resentment, or jealousy. In our unwillingness to forgive before God, we become the issue.[3]

It's helpful to see ourselves lifting this sin and all its consequences to God, to see ourselves laying the entire deal in his hands. Does this take trust? You bet it does. That's why we're on the road of Trusting God. In an act of trust, we hand over the responsibility of what to do next to our fully wise, good, trustworthy, and just Lord. We fully acknowledge the wrong done to us, and we place both the act and the consequences into his hands. The whole incident—the facts, thoughts, feelings, judgments, and resulting pain—moves out of our sphere into God's.

How will we know if we've forgiven someone? When we know we can offer that person our love. When forgiveness stays only in our minds and doesn't sink deep into our hearts, it cannot be effective.

Like repentance, forgiveness is a matter of the heart. The act genuinely clears the mind and emotions of sin and all its effects in us. Bill forgave his friends before God long before he hired them to work for him and had that face-to-face meeting. On that day *they* received his forgiveness. But Bill had experienced the benefits of forgiving them long before they heard him say, "I forgive you."

When we forgive, first vertically and then horizontally, it's like huge cement bags have been lifted off our shoulders. It makes us ready to love again, and that prepares us for the next key.

KEY #5: Forgive the Offender When They Repent, for Their Sake

Forgiving the person before God releases us of judgment, bitterness, and resentment toward our offender. When we forgive, our heart heals and we are ready to forgive the one who hurt us—person to person—for that person's sake.

Whew, doggies! This is one of those incredible times when the benefits of trusting God are visibly and profoundly mysterious and miraculous. Such is the miracle of God's grace in our heart.

Yet to go to another and declare "I forgive you" before that person repents does nothing for the relationship and robs the offender of the opportunity for his or her own life-freeing repentance. God uses repentance to heal sinful hearts. We shouldn't deprive our offender of that gift. Our forgiveness will not free the other person from their offense, nor will it heal our relationship, if it is premature. The one who sinned against us must repent for his or her own sake—to be healed from sin. Upon the other person's repentance, we can forgive.

We forgive our offender with the goal of restoring the relationship, not just resolving the conflict. We desire our offender's repentance, not to hold it over him or her, but so we can continue on in a healthy relationship. Their repentance won't heal our heart—that is what happens when we forgive our offender before God. But their repentance will heal our *relationship*.

We can pursue reconciliation, but we can't force it. We can't demand repentance. As you may remember from chapter 5, repentance requires a heart that trusts God. That's a grace-room moment. Our insistence that another repent has no sway in the matter.

Have you ever noticed that Jesus waits for our repentance before he forgives us? Think about it. On the cross he cried out, "Father, forgive them."[4] If that cry was for *our* sake, then everyone gets forgiven, receives salvation, and goes to heaven, regardless of their decision of repentance. We know that isn't the case. On the cross Jesus asked the Father to forgive those who had crucified him, for *his* own sake, that he would not be contaminated by the sin done against him. Jesus on the cross demonstrates key number four. When we repent of our sins against God and ask for his forgiveness, then and only then does he forgive us and reconcile us to himself. When we repent, Jesus grants forgiveness for our sake.

When we forgive the offender, for his or her sake, it prepares the way for the relationship to be restored.

When we allow God to heal us from being sinned against, we get to turn around and help those who have sinned against us to find healing from their sin! How amazing!

KEY #6: Distinguish Between Forgiving and Trusting Your Offender

As forgiveness prepares the way for the relationship to be restored, it is important to understand that forgiveness does not mean we have to trust the other person yet. This misunderstanding causes many to balk at forgiveness. Because they can't trust the person, they believe they can't forgive him or her. But forgiving the person and trusting the person again are always separate issues. Even if we have forgiven our offender—even if our offender has repented and asked our forgiveness—we will still, in the future, have to deal with the issue of mutual trust. Trustworthiness must be evaluated. Our expectations should be realistic because while trust is easily broken, it is recovered very slowly, and sometimes not at all. Forgiveness carries the hope of renewed trust in the offender, but it does not mandate or guarantee it. For example, when sin violates the commitment of marriage, the offender can be and should be forgiven, but the restoration of the trust necessary to re-honor the commitment takes time.

KEY #7: Seek Reconciliation, Not Just Conflict Resolution

When we help someone say, "Will you forgive me?" we engage that person in the relationship. Reconciliation belongs to a completely different stratosphere than mere conflict resolution. Most of us want to settle for just fixing the conflict. So we use terms like, "I'm sorry that happened," or "I really made a mistake on that one." When we are willing to say, "Will you forgive me because I did _____?" we create the opportunity for people to forgive us and sometimes even come back into heart relationship with us.

As recreation director at a day-care center, John felt like he was the Henry Kissinger of playground diplomacy when he forced two eight-year-old boys in conflict to apologize to each other. In his most authoritative playground director's voice, John said, "All right, what happened here?" Not a great question to ask if you want an honest answer. (What would you answer? "Well, sir, I cheated at baseball and called Kevin out when he was safe. Then I hit him in the leg with the baseball bat. Before he had a chance to react I got him in a headlock and was about to gouge his eyes out when you showed up.")

After listening to both of their versions, which were oddly different, and after hearing a dozen distinct versions from the assembled mob, John recalls, "I knew I would not be able to render a just verdict, so I said, 'All right, Trevor. I want you to apologize to Kevin. And Kevin, I want you to forgive Trevor.' They looked at me as though I had said, 'Kids, I want you to find a mule and take it bowling.' Solitary confinement they could have understood and obeyed. Sweeping the breezeway for a year would have made sense. But apologizing and forgiving? On what basis? Neither was sorry and neither was ready to forgive someone who wasn't sorry.

"But their lack of readiness didn't stop me. I pushed, saying, 'I mean it—now!' Trevor mumbled, 'I'm sorry,' and Kevin muttered, 'I forgive you.' By forcing them to do something they didn't believe, I caused them to betray themselves. And, by forcing a request for insincere forgiveness, I kept these kids from honestly facing what they had done wrong. I kept them both from an opportunity to be made right with the other."

In our anxiousness to fix conflicts, we sometimes push people to say they are sorry. But have you noticed that people don't get fixed or stay fixed when we try to force it? Grace always invites rather than demands reconciliation. An apology may make the issue go away for the present time, but it won't heal the relationship. Remember—that's what forgiveness always seeks. Jesus paid with his life to bring us reconciliation. This is sacred ground.

Mystery in The Room of Grace

A distinguished draftsman, engineer, artist, and thinker, Leonardo da Vinci is one of the outstanding intellects of history. Just before he started painting *The Last Supper*, he had a violent quarrel with a fellow painter. Enraged and bitter, Leonardo determined to paint the face of his enemy—the other artist—as the face of Judas and thus take out his revenge by sending this man down in infamy. Judas was one of the first faces he painted, and everyone recognized the face of the painter with whom Leonardo had quarreled.

But when Leonardo came to paint the face of Christ, he could make no progress. Something was holding him back, frustrating his best efforts. Eventually, he came to the conclusion that the thing checking and frustrating him was that he had painted his enemy as Judas. He decided to paint out the face of Judas and start fresh on the face of Jesus. He did, and this time with the success which the ages have acclaimed.[5]

Leonardo experienced the power and genius of grace. He had discovered a universal truth: We cannot simultaneously paint the features of Christ into our life and paint another face with the colors of enmity and hatred.

Where does God stand in relation to the sin done against us when we live in The Room of Grace? He stands with us. He has his arm around us, giving us his perspective on the sin and the one who sinned. He's close enough for us to hear him say, "If you ask me—and I hope you do—you should forgive this person as my Son forgave you. Trust me with this advice, and I'll heal you, restore you, and free you with the truth it brings to you."

God stands with us in The Room of Grace because we trusted him. He says, "You believe that I have made you a saint. Now, live as one. My Son died to reconcile you. That was my ultimate Gift to you. It made possible this mysterious power—the gift of forgiveness. Please value it as I do. Forgive those who have sinned against you."

God has given us three gifts beyond explaining. The best gift we can give back to God is our trust.[6] Trust him with the forgiveness issues in your life.

—≡ DID YOU DISCOVER?

- The powerful gift of forgiveness has one main purpose: to protect us from the insidious harm that comes from *sin done against us*.

- God's provision for our healing always begins with our recognition that someone has sinned against us.

- There is a sequence for forgiveness to resolve sin.

- To forgive, we must first admit what is already true.

- We forgive the offenders in our lives for what they've done and its consequences in our life. This is between God and us, for our sake.

- Forgiving others for the consequences of their sin against us is usually much more difficult than the sin itself.

- Forgiving the person before God releases us of judgment, bitterness, and resentment toward our offender.

- We forgive our offender with the goal of restoring the relationship, not just resolving the conflict.

- When we forgive the offender for his or her sake, it prepares the way for the relationship to be restored.

- Forgiveness carries the hope of renewed trust in the relationship, but it does not mandate or guarantee it. Forgiving and trusting are not the same thing.

- Grace always invites rather than demands reconciliation.

CHAPTER SEVEN

Maturing into God's Dreams for You

For the longest time I used to think that my major contribution to the body of Christ would be my attendance at potlucks.

—Bob Ryan

$\overline{\overline{}}$. . . **A**nd then the day comes. For some, the release feels premature; for others, the wait is agonizingly long. But all have learned to believe the day would arrive. Life in The Room of Grace teaches us to wait for God's exaltation rather than to pursue position or power.[1] The timing is perfect. For one thing, our dreams are being clarified as our sin is being resolved, our wounds are being healed, and we are in the process of maturing. Our lives are no longer about proving our worth to others through what we get to do.

And then one day the "whys" stop. Why has it taken so long? Why did so many revisions of that dream have to die or be rerouted all those years? For on that day a mature friend escorts you to the far back of the room, telling you only this, "We all knew this day was coming. I am so proud of you." Your friend drops you off at what looks like a train station. A fog of steam reveals only the outline of someone standing just outside an arch with the words Dreams and Destiny written across it.

You approach the arch and discover the figure is a Ticket Giver with one ticket in his hand. He smiles kindly and broadly, puts his hands on your shoulders, and looks into your eyes for quite a while before speaking. When he does, you suddenly realize the Ticket Giver is the same person who handed you those grace gifts all along. As he hands you the ticket, he tells you that this day was prepared before the world began. He tells you that this moment couldn't have been forced or rushed or manipulated to come one second sooner. He tells you that he loves you as much as his Father loves him.

Then he hugs you and hands you the ticket. He tells you that this destiny was created specially for you.[2] And then he ushers you away with the words, "Now hurry up and get on that train. A whole lot of folk are waiting for you to walk into this destiny and into their lives."[3]

And you walk through the arch into the world you were designed and prepared for. The time has come to do much of what you were placed on this earth for. You never stop returning to The Room of Grace, for your heart and protection reside there. But now you get to draw others into The Room of Grace. That's what this dream is ultimately about—your place in God's kingdom.

Philip Yancey asks, "Is it absurd to believe that one human being, a tiny dot on a tiny planet, can make a difference in the history of the universe?"[4] According to the Bible, that's exactly how God designed the kingdom—this staging ground for the battle of the universe—to work. It's a kingdom where God uses healing and maturing people to bring his grace to hopeless and hurting people. You get to use your gifts, passion, and healed heart to show the glory of Jesus, who has loved you beyond telling from the beginning of time.

Throughout this book, we've been painting a picture of the broken, fragile, unusable, and even the competently miserable coming to the end of their striving and growing into maturity in the The Room of Grace. As we've said all along, God's goal for us is never just healing, safety, rest, or even receiving love, as astounding and stunning as those gifts are. His goal is that we be released into these dreams we've not been able to shake all of our lives. Remember the opening lines of this book? "Ever since we were children we have had dreams and hopes of destiny. Some of these dreams are our own, but others came from the very hand of God—and God's dreams never go off the radar screen. Even time, failure, or heartbreak can't make us forget them entirely. Still, most of us have tried to stuff them into the attic. We have been rudely awakened out of too many of them, too many times, and each time we lost more and more of the dream. Yet even if we've forgotten the fiber of those dreams, God has not."

We also promised, God has a ticket of destiny with your name written on it—no matter how old, how broken, how tired, or how frightened you are. No matter how many times you may have failed, God dearly longs for the day when he gets to hand you that ticket, smile, and whisper into your ear, "You have no idea how long I've waited to hand this to you. Have a blast! I've already seen what you get to do. It's better than you could have dreamed. Now hurry up and get on that train. A whole lot of folk are waiting for you to walk into your destiny and into their lives."

The Room of Grace prepares you for that unspeakable day of release because in this room you are in the process of maturing. In this chapter we want to offer a few crucial observations on maturity, specifically what hinders it and what promotes it. Then we will introduce you to two friends who have met the ticket puncher in the back of The Room of Grace, where trains leave all the time, taking us into God's dream for us.

All aboard!

What Hinders God's Dream for Us?

People in The Room of Good Intentions never get released into the dreams God has for them. Everyone here is trying to change into someone else to appease God. We hide, position, strive, perfect our self-effort, and polish our image. We often interpret our ability to compete well against each other as a sign of our godliness and success. We look very impressive—we have learned to package our techniques well—but our self-effort keeps us self-centered and immature.

As we said in chapter 2, whenever we are trapped in shame or blame or anger, for any period of time, we stop maturing. This is what happens when we lodge in The Room of Good Intentions. We may become competent and skilled. We may achieve position and significant-looking roles. We do stuff—maybe even impressive stuff. But, because we are constantly pursuing power and authority, and manipulating to gain control, God can never release us into our future. Our relational sadness, our inability to be loved, our festering wounds and broken relationships freeze us in immaturity. Without humility, we continue to miss the train that takes us into God's intention for our destiny.

There is no *releasing* without *maturing.*

There is no maturing without *healing.*

There is no healing without *gifts of grace.*

There are no gifts of grace outside The Room of Grace.

There is no Room of Grace without a door marked Living Out of Who God Says I Am, opened with a doorknob of Humility.

There is no humility without choosing to walk a road called Trusting God.

Only then do I learn how God stands with me to resolve my sin.

Growing into Maturity in The Room of Grace

We who dwell in The Room of Grace have come to believe who God says we are. We're not trying to change into another person. God has made us exactly who he wants us to be, and we have come to believe it. Any change that takes place in us comes from maturing into the person we already are—much like a caterpillar matures into a butterfly.

Jesus is the Son of God. As man, he matured in God's perfect timing for release into the astonishing destiny God had for him. Jesus did not try to change to be better in order to please his Father. He already knew that his Father was well pleased with him.[5] Instead, he constantly entrusted himself to the Father so that he could mature.[6] We are told to emulate Jesus' pattern of entrusting himself to his Father.[7]

In The Room of Grace we learn to trust, to wait, to rest in God's promises, to grow in health and authentic relationships, so we will mature toward the day of God's releasing us into our destiny.[8] We don't pursue power, authority, or office. We wait to receive God's authority, his exaltation of the humble. We patiently wait for God to give us the desires of our hearts.[9] We're no longer in a hurry. We know he cares about our destiny more than we do. We know he has already seen the day of our release. It makes us smile, like remembering a secret shared between best friends.

The mature in this room have also learned how to live with a community of people who trust God and others with what is true about them. We—and the others in this community—have taken off our masks and are learning to walk in the resplendent freedom and purposes of God. But we remember the pain of letting go of our masks; we still carry the scars from where the glue tore our skin.

We are not free from visible problems and issues just because we no longer hide them. Our issues are there for everyone to see. Sometimes the mature homeowners in The Room of Grace appear to have more issues than the prize citizens of The Room of Good Intentions.

We depend upon God and his power and resources. We are free to trust him for repentance. We are free to trust him so we can forgive others and be forgiven.

Most of all, the mature have a childlike joy and freedom. We are playfully alive and will never allow anyone to return us to hiding. We may be tempted to stumble back into the empty promises of The Room of Good Intentions, but that lure carries less and less power as we mature in The Room of Grace. We have tasted too much life to want to leave this room. We know too much; we've drunk deeply of the grace of God. It has blanketed us like wool and hot cocoa on a cold night. We are part of the growing neighborhood of those who've chosen to believe who God says we are.

But such maturity does not happen overnight. God uses many others for our benefit in this process. Some are teachers, counselors, friends, pastors, spouses, siblings, children, mentors, disciplers, spiritual guides, and spiritual directors.[10]

Spiritual disciplines are practiced in The Room of Grace as part of the process of maturing and releasing the saint to minister the gospel of the kingdom. These disciplines are no longer seen as a means of entry to The Room of Grace. "They are disciplines designed to help us be active and effective in the spiritual realm of our own heart, now spiritually alive by grace in relationship to God and his kingdom."[11]

Growing in Maturity

Maturity in The Room of Grace occurs in three general phases. Of course, these phases overlap each other, and we often jump back and forth in our development. But for the sake of clarity, we are making each phase more distinct than it actually is in experience.

Phase One: Healing the Needy Christian

As we have pointed out, everyone who walks into The Room of Grace initially is me-centered. In this room we learn some foundational, essential truths: We become acquainted with the power of love and grace and truth; we identify the various wounds we carry; we embrace the significance of our new identity; we discover relational principles. We also discover the process of unresolved sin issues as well as the cycle and power of sin. We are immersed in the person and work of Jesus, the Holy Spirit, and the Father.

But if we remain in this phase, we will stagnate and grow cynical because we are not applying the truths we are learning. We need not rush through this phase, however; it's important not to force application before we understand what we are applying. Such is a breeding ground for self-effort.

One of the greatest gifts we can offer another person is a safe place to fail. In this room, teachers and mentors help youthful followers of Christ to learn the priority of not hiding. This is such a place—a room where they can disclose what is really true about the sin in them and the sin that has been done against them. Such a gift at this phase in a believer's life is profound and freeing.

Young, maturing believers adapt themselves to others' expectations, real or imagined. So we want to make sure our expectations match God's expectations. If they don't and others try to meet our inappropriate expectations, we actually thwart their maturity. So we model and teach truth about who they are in Christ; who God says they are. As you know by now, it isn't enough to know what the Bible says about who we are in Christ. We must actually live it. We do well to hang around real people who are living it. This is how we nurture maturity in another.

Phase Two: Maturing the Healing Christian

In time we become more others-centered. In the previous stage, the emphasis was on introduction and new awareness of truth. In this stage we focus with others on applying, developing, and processing the truths we learned in phase one. For example, we learn to apply love, grace, and truth to our life situation and circumstances, and so our wounds begin to heal. We begin living out of our new identity and applying truth to the dynamics of sin. We begin to experience in real relationships the relational principles we are learning, and we understand that what we are learning is not just something we know, but something we are experiencing as truth. We are developing a vitally wonderful relationship with Jesus, the Holy Spirit, and the Father. In this phase, we are looking around our world and beyond to see how God wants us to love others.

This stage more fully introduces the reality of suffering. Not the suffering from sickness, accidents, or unfortunate circumstances, but the suffering that comes from aligning ourselves with truth, with truth-telling. God uses suffering to mature the humble as they come under his influence and obey his truth, out of a heart of love. As they grow in trust during this suffering, God will enlarge their sphere of influence, because the humble can be trusted with truth.

At this stage we are looking for and encouraging vulnerability, made evident by our new level of authenticity. We no longer hide. We don't arrive at this stage by taking an eight-week series or a class. Maturity is a process; it takes time. Don't rush the pace it takes for character to mature.

Phase Three: Releasing the Maturing Christian

In this third stage, our life becomes more Christ-centered. We naturally respond to life out of our new identity—a Christlike identity—that we live through grace and truth. Our past wounds no longer identify us, and we experience freedom in our new identity. We no longer live under the control of sin. We are experiencing the power of community and relational vulnerability. And, maybe best of all, we live as an intimate friend of Jesus. We mature into a beautiful, trusting dependency upon the Holy Spirit and walk into the purposes of God the Father. In this stage we are looking around our world and beyond to see how God wants us to love others through his particular plans and destiny for us.

We gauge maturity by how we live with others who are maturing. Mature Christians delight in God's exaltation of others. We do not fear others' strengths; we understand them, submit to them, and benefit from them. The mature influence others, not so much out of the power of their position, but out of their person. We receive power; we don't pursue it. We focus on influence, not on opportunities that might compromise our convictions.

We make decisions primarily for the benefit of others and are willing to suffer so that others might mature. We receive our destiny from God's hand. We learn to own and take responsibility for our influence. We accept the cost of commitment that comes with someone trusting us. The mature enjoy God's protection and his jealous love for them. We offer to others that same kind of protective love and receive it from others. The mature ask the exhilarating question fashioned by Ken Gire, "What dream is God dreaming when He dreams about you and about me, and how can we help that dream come true?"[12] The mature are always learning, studying, and inviting others to speak into our lives and meet our needs.[13]

Does this sound too good to be true? Believe us — it is not. In fact, it even gets better.

Unlikely Dreamers

Kit and Bob are but two examples of individuals living out of God's dreams for them, dreams of destiny and hope. We'd like to tell you their stories so you can see what God can do with unlikely dreamers who choose to walk the path of Trusting God and start living in The Room of Grace.

Kit has been called the Mother Teresa of Phoenix for her twenty-plus years of unswerving commitment to those living in the city's cycle of poverty. She now stewards a godly vision that engages the lives of hundreds who minister to thousands. Kit speaks nationally to the holistic needs of the poor, to the development of indigenous leaders, to the lifelong commitments necessary to break the cycle of poverty.

Her commitment to Christ as a teenager came in the middle of her family's greatest crisis: her mother's alcoholism and her father's suicide. A teenager from a wealthy family, Kit was immersed in the world of affluence, social standing, and notoriety. She became a debutante and prom queen. When her father died, she didn't know how to take the pain and shame anywhere but inward. As her mother's alcoholism continued to distort life, Kit learned how to form a mask to wear in her fashionably public world. She so wanted her happy-looking life to run smoothly. She wore a bright smile and a confident demeanor, but inside she was hiding and full of pain.

Her mask said, "I am competent enough." And she nearly was. Exceptionally bright and intelligent, she was mature beyond her years in many areas. In college she headed a number of campus ministries and already had a strong voice in civil rights issues. She was driven, focused, on-track, and filled with vision and immense capacity. And full of the Inevitable Effects of unresolved hurt and guilt.

Then she met Wayne. He introduced her to a family of believers who, although impressed by her talents and abilities, were committed to ministering to her person, to her heart. Despite Kit's accomplishments, her heart needed healing, her issues needing resolving, and her character needed maturing. Within this family, Kit learned the incredible principles of trust, grace, and humility. She began to trust God and others with who she was and with their strengths to meet her needs, especially her needs for protection and love. As she began healing and maturing she also learned that her dreams were God's dreams for her. And, in time, he chose to release her into a vision even beyond her wildest dreams. She had once been a profoundly articulate influencer with an immense dream and prophetic message, headed for the "shallow grave" of disillusionment, burnout, and "train wrecks." Now she is that prophetic influencer, but protected within a community where she is trusted, known, and wonderfully loved. The results have been nothing short of breathtaking.

Kit knows that God released her into this dream, and this gives her confidence in his faithfulness to protect her in the darkest corners of the city. He provided her a place where she and others could learn through trust the incredible value of every person. It has freed her to live and minister out of who God has designed her to be.

For one day, years ago, some friends took Kit by the hand and ushered her to the far back of The Room of Grace. There she was handed a note by the Ticket Giver, which read: "Kit, this is what I will do with you. I will now use you to give hope to the hopeless, love to the unloved, freedom to the captives, justice to the victims. I will give you the city. Wherever you put your hand, children and adults will come to be healed and given life. I will give you land in the heart of the city, and I will create a campus where people will be taught to minister to the needy. You will call it Neighborhood Ministries. Now hurry up and get on that train. A whole lot of folk are waiting for you to walk into this destiny and into their lives."

And that day, Kit fell to her knees and wept, overcome with grace and love. Overcome with a life beyond her wildest dreams. As she stood up, she looked back, smiled at the Ticket Giver, and started running to the train.

Bob is one of the actors, directors, and writers for a ministry that has been reaching his city through award-winning drama performed at its finest theaters. Bob also is a highly gifted songwriter who is finishing his first CD.

Most would agree, however, that he had no business coming to this place in life. Bob had violated himself and the people he loved most in this world so many times that many had given up on him. He had harbored no hope of ever being free—it seemed that he would only and always be what he was guilty of doing. Most of his Christian life Bob has been deeply troubled with some very significant and severe issues of unresolved relational sin. He has spent years in therapy. But twelve years ago, he stepped into an environment where he was, for the first time, free to be honest about who he is.

Bob actually discovered and chose to enter The Room of Grace. Don't be fooled. During these years, he has fallen back into the darkness of hidden duplicity more than once. But people he has grown to trust in The Room of Grace will not let him go. It may be hard to imagine that a person could be in The Room of Grace and still stumble around, failing and failed, for seasons at a time. But that is what The Room of Grace is all about. For God's grace is perfected in our imperfection. The Room of Grace is not a place where we do not sin. The Room of Grace is where we are protected by those who love us . . . people we have learned to trust with the deepest part of our pain, ugliness, fear, and failure.

Today, Bob understands, more than most of us, that he is a man loved by God. He now clearly trusts an identity in Christ that has become his lifeline. Yet he remains daily aware of how prone he is to engage, at any moment, in unhealthy behavior. Bob continues to struggle with sin, but when he trusted that he was actually who God said he was, he realized he could also be honest about all of who he is. Finding others he could trust with himself helped Bob to experience profound healing. Now he lives in a humble realization that in spite of what is true about him, he does not have to be a victim of his own, sometimes sinful, choices. He is by faith who God says he is, even on his worst day. Yet, in his humility, he never denies that he is capable of great wrong—and he has proven this more than once in The Room of Grace. But Love will not let him go.

We will never forget the night Bob sang a song for John's fiftieth birthday party. That night he sat in front of eighty or so people. These were the ones Love used to bring him to a fragile but profound life of beautiful relationships and ministry, form-fitted to match his passion and gifts. Bob will always be one bad alley away from failure, but Bob is alive. God receives much glory in lives like Bob's.

Fiddling with a few notes, Bob started to sing and then abruptly stopped. He took a deep breath and then spoke to these friends words that had taken decades to form: "My friendship with you brought me into an environment where I was not discarded. I am known among this warm gathering of rabble. I am so astonished that I have been given these last few years of hope. These verses are to thank God, who has given them to me." And then he filled the night sky with this most beautiful song.

Sometimes By Faith

The morning stumbles in,
Lights a candle for the night gone by,
Rubs its weary eyes,
Wipes a tear out of the dreary skies.

Soft is the morning light, gone is the troubled night;
The dark dreams fade.

Birds in the morning sing,
A new day filtering in through the shade.

As long as dreams follow the day,
As long as light gives way to night,
God knows that you and I will walk this way:
Sometimes by faith, sometimes by sight.

When darkness settles in,
Everything we know can tend to slip away.
Things we swore we believed shiver into mist
And vanish in the gray.

The night falls hard and cold,
Dredging up all those old familiar scenes.
But look at how the morning breaks;
Think about how time can shake up everything.

As long as dreams follow the day,
As long as light gives way to night,
God knows that you and I will walk this way:
Sometimes by faith, sometimes by sight.

The morning stumbles in, lights a candle for the night gone by.
Grace draws a streak of gold across the black wall of the eastern sky.[14]

For one day, years ago, some friends took Bob by the hand and ushered him to the far back of The Room of Grace. They dropped him off and said: "We all knew this day was coming. We are so proud of you." As he approached an arch with the words Dreams and Destiny written across it, he discovered that the figure giving out tickets was the one who handed him those grace gifts all along. That day the Ticket Giver smiled kindly and broadly on Bob, put his hands on Bob's shoulders, and looked into his eyes for quite some time. He spoke some words for only the two of them. And then he handed Bob a ticket with this written on it: "Bob, this is what I will do with you. I want you to take drama into this city. I want you to use all the gifts I've prepared in you to tell them of my love in a way they can understand. I am sending you to the Herberger Theater, the most important performing arts center in the city. Have a blast. Now hurry up and get on that train. A whole lot of folk are waiting for you to walk into this destiny and into their lives."

On that day, Bob fell to his knees and wept, overcome with grace and love. Overcome with a life beyond his wildest dreams. As he stood up, he looked back, smiled at the Ticket Giver, and started running to the train.

A New Kind of Performer

In chapter 1 we said, "We are all performers, but because of sin we've lost confidence that we will always please our audience, and so we put on a mask. As an unintended result, no one, not even the people I love, ever get to see my true face. The real me."

We are all performers. One question remains: Will you perform to gain the acceptance and pleasure of your audience—and always feel that you have failed? Or will you perform out of a heart of trusting delight, knowing you have already pleased your Audience?

The offer of a life in The Room of Grace is not conjecture or wishful thinking. It is not religious consolation or an untried utopian state where no one lives. Many people all over this world live there. The play has been written; the good works have already been created for us to walk in.[15] We are believing who God says we are, and we are actually choosing to trust it in spite of what we act out every day. We are astonished by the reality that a life beyond appearances can truly be ours. In grace, God has made it possible for us to live *True-Faced* . . . and he is grinning widely in excited anticipation to do the same for you.

≡ DID YOU DISCOVER?

- There is no releasing without maturing. There is no maturing without healing. There is no healing without gifts of grace. There are no gifts of grace outside The Room of Grace. There is no Room of Grace without a door marked Living Out of Who God Says I Am, opened with a doorknob of Humility. There is no humility without choosing to walk a road called Trusting God. Only then do I learn how God stands with me to resolve my sin.

- In The Room of Grace we learn to trust, to wait, to rest in God's promises. As this causes us to grow in health and authentic relationships, we will mature toward the day of God's releasing us into our destiny.

- We—and the others in this community of grace—have taken off our masks and are learning to walk in the resplendent freedom and purposes of God.

- One of the greatest gifts we can offer another person is a safe place to fail.

- God uses suffering to mature the humble as they come under his influence and obey his truth, out of a heart of love.

- The mature influence others, not so much out of the power of their position, but out of their person.

- We learn to take responsibility for our influence.

- Life in The Room of Grace teaches us to wait for God's exaltation, rather than to pursue position or power.

Notes

Chapter One

1. 1 Samuel 13.
2. Genesis 3:9-10, NASB.
3. See Genesis 3:7-11.
4. 1 Corinthians 6:9-11. Paul speaks of those among the Corinthian believers who were "fornicators," "idolaters," "adulterers," "effeminate," "homosexuals," on so on, and how they were "washed," "sanctified," and "justified in the name of the Lord Jesus and in the Spirit of our God." However, the important point here is that they all knew these things about themselves—each and every one of them knew the background of each and every other one! They were definitely not living in the Land of "Doing Just Fine."
5. See Revelation 3:17. Some of you may be thinking, "Well, I definitely don't think we are in the Laodicean period!" Whatever your eschatological views about Revelation 2–3, please recall that the seven churches to whom John wrote on behalf of Christ himself were seven actual churches in seven actual cities in Asia Minor. The question to ask yourself is, "Do I sound like the Laodiceans with their smug self-sufficiency?"
6. Psalm 51:3-14.
7. Psalm 31:12; 41:7-10; 52:2-4; Proverbs 15:4; 26:28; 27:4.
8. 1 Samuel 25:18-35.
9. See James 1:22-23.
10. 2 Corinthians 3:18.

Chapter Two

1. Matthew 5:48. See also Leviticus 19:2; Deuteronomy 18:13; 1 Peter 1:14-16.

2. Romans 5:8; Matthew 28:20b; Hebrews 13:5; Acts 18:9-10.

3. Hebrews 11:6. The word "faith" is the noun form of the word "believe" or "trust." Note the connection here.

4. Philippians 3:9. Not only does it disregard the righteousness we already have in Christ, but it explicitly contradicts the principle Paul enunciates in Galatians 3:1-3 and Colossians 2:6; that is, that we received Christ by faith and that is also how we are to live in him!

5. Galatians 2:16-18, MSG.

6. Genesis 4:4-5. The problem was not just the offering, but something was wrong within the motive of Cain himself.

7. 1 Samuel 13:5-15; Hebrews 3:18-19; 4:2. The link between trust and obedience is unmistakable.

8. I am blessed, Ephesians 1:3; I am chosen and holy, 1:4; I am adopted, 1:5; I am forgiven, 1:7; I am favored, 1:7-8; I am close to God, 2:13; I am loved, 3:17-19; I am promised great things, 3:6; I am cherished, 5:29.

9. Ephesians 1:3-14.

10. Galatians 6:15, MSG.

11. Proverbs 3:5-6.

12. Matthew 7:15-16, MSG.

13. Erwin McManus, *An Unstoppable Force* (Loveland, Colo.: Group Publishing, 2001), p. 156.

14. Galatians 3:5, MSG.

15. Revelation 3:15-22. The word in verse 16 literally is "vomit" rather than "spit," as it is often more politely translated. Politeness, however, masks God's revulsion with such lukewarm self-sufficience!

16. Colossians 1:10-12, NASB.

17. Romans 12:1-2. Paul specifically references the truth taught earlier in this chapter in that the word he uses for "transformed" is a form of the Greek verb from which we get "metamorphosis," which is nothing other than the process of maturing into what you were designed to be!

18. Philippians 4:18.

19. 1 Thessalonians 4:1.

20. Ephesians 3:20-21.

Chapter Three

1. 1 Peter 5:5-6.

2. 1 Peter 5:5-6.

3. Galatians 5:1.

4. 2 Corinthians 12:9-10. When I recognize my own weakness, my own inability, I allow the power of Christ to be seen in me. Until I do, it is hidden by my own abilities, my own talents, my own efforts, my own pride!

5. For a more complete description of our new identity in Christ, see Henry Holloman, *The Forgotten Blessing* (Nashville: Word, 1999), chapter 3, pp. 25-40.

6. Galatians 5:1-4.

7. Deuteronomy 31:6; Hebrews 13:5.

8. Romans 8:1-4. The Law could not make us free of condemnation, for we will always fall short of it in some respect. God did make us free of condemnation, for the blood of Jesus paid for every way in which we fall short of God's character.

9. Hebrews 4:16.

10. John 1:14-18.

11. John 13:34-35.

12. J. R. R. Tolkien, *The Fellowship of the Ring* (New York: Houghton Mifflin, 1954), p. 218.

13. Romans 8:28; 1 Peter 1:3-5.

14. Galatians 5:1.

15. Psalm 78:72; Galatians 5:6,13-14; 1 Timothy 3:1-7.

16. Romans 8:28-30. God loves us so much that he wants us to be just like Jesus.

17. Jeremiah 1:5; 1 Peter 5:5-6. You may say, "But I can't be a prophet to the nations like Jeremiah!" Perhaps not, but God has plans for you that are equally stunning. See Jeremiah 29:11 and Isaiah 25:1.

18. Psalm 37:4; Proverbs 3:5-6.

19. 2 Corinthians 3:18.

Chapter Four

1. 1 John 4:19.
2. James 2:18; 3:13. Rick Warren explains that spiritual maturity is demonstrated more by behavior than by stated beliefs. Rick Warren, *The Purpose Driven Church* (Grand Rapids, Mich.: Zondervan, 1999), pp. 336-338.
3. Genesis 2:18–3:9.
4. John 13:5-20.
5. Romans 5:5,8.
6. Zephaniah 3:17.
7. Lamentations 3:32-33. The underlying concept of *hesed* is that of "loyal love" or "covenant love." It is epitomized in Jeremiah 31:3: "I have loved you with an everlasting love; therefore I have drawn you with lovingkindness." (NASB)
8. Hebrews 12:6.
9. Psalm 33:4; 119:160; Hebrews 6:18.
10. Exodus 34:14-15; Hosea 11:1-12.
11. 1 Timothy 1:12.
12. 1 Samuel 18–19. Saul feared, and therefore mistrusted, David. Since he did not trust him, he refused the love and loyalty that David clearly offered him. Contrast this with Jonathan's willingness to trust David and the love he received—and offered—as a result.
13. Ephesians 5:21. And, according to verses 18-20, it is evidence of a Spirit-filled life.
14. *Jekyll & Hyde, The Musical,* Act One. Even those who may not know Christ understand the truth of this common grace which requires trusting relationships.
15. 1 John 4:18.
16. 2 Timothy 2:13; Deuteronomy 7:7-9. Not only will he not let us down, he cannot, because to do so would violate his very nature. He is the ultimately trustworthy one. He cannot act against his own nature since to do so would be to deny who he is—something he could never do, because he only operates in the realm of truth.
17. Isaiah 53:4-6. The ultimate grace-giver was the most beaten up of all! And in his case, he deserved none of it!

18. *Webster's New Collegiate Dictionary* (Springfield, Mass.: G&C Merriam Co., 1972).

Chapter Five

1. Luke 18:14.
2. 1 John 1:7. The verb "cleanses" is present tense. It carries the sense of "goes on cleansing." As we walk with him in the light, his blood goes on cleansing us from all sin!
3. Isaiah 64:6. The word translated "filthy rags" (or similar phrase, depending upon the translation) is actually the word for "cast off menstrual cloths." They represented the lack of life.
4. *Webster's New Collegiate Dictionary* (Springfield, Mass.: G&C Merriam Co., 1972).
5. Colossians 2:6.
6. Titus 3:4-6.
7. 2 Corinthians 7:10-11.
8. Henry and Richard Blackaby, *Spiritual Leadership* (Nashville: Broadman & Holman, 2001), p. 237. See also Proverbs 16:18.
9. 2 Samuel 6:6-7.
10. Romans 2:4. Paul says that it is the riches of God's kindness, tolerance, and patience that lead us to repentance. Not the fear of punishment. Not self-striving. God's kindness! How sweet indeed!
11. Brennan Manning, *The Ragamuffin Gospel* (Sisters, Oreg.: Multnomah, 1990), p. 154.

Chapter Six

1. 2 Samuel 13. Examine Absalom's response to the hurt done to his sister by Amnon: "But Absalom did not speak to Amnon either good or bad; for Absalom hated Amnon because he had violated his sister Tamar" (v. 22). Then he proceeded to plot and carry out Amnon's death! This offense also set up the heart attitude of Absalom that later issued in his rebellion against his father David.
2. Ephesians 4:32.
3. Read Jesus' astonishing words recorded in Matthew 6:12-15. He actually ties our ability to be forgiven by God to our willingness to forgive the sins of others against us! If we harbor unforgiveness in

our hearts toward others, how can we even pretend that we are truly desirous of his forgiveness toward us? He has surely forgiven us of far more than we could ever be asked to forgive others of, has he not?

4. Luke 23:34.

5. C. E. MacCartney, as cited by Paul Lee Tan, ed., *Encyclopedia: Signs of the Times* (Rockville, Md.: Assurance Publishers, 1979), p. 457.

6. 1 Peter 1:7-8. If you replace the words "faith" and "believe" (as they are in most translations) with the single word "trust," you'll see the impact of this more fully.

Chapter Seven

1. 1 Peter 5:5-6.

2. Ephesians 2:10. God has tailor-made good works for you to perform! They're out there waiting just for you.

3. Jeremiah 29:11. God delivered this promise to Israel even after seventy years of exile in Babylon! He still had remarkable plans for them. He does for you, too.

4. Philip Yancey, *Disappointment with God* (Grand Rapids, Mich.: Zondervan, 1988), p. 169.

5. Matthew 3:17.

6. Hebrews 5:7-10; 1 Peter 2:21-23.

7. Philippians 2:5-11; 1 Peter 4:19.

8. Psalm 37:7; 40:4; 1 Peter 5:5-6.

9. Psalm 37:4.

10. Bruce Demarest, *Soul Guide* (Colorado Springs, Colo.: NavPress, 2003), p. 40.

11. Dallas Willard, *The Divine Conspiracy* (San Francisco: HarperSanFrancisco, 1998), pp. 353, 418.

12. Ken Gire, *Windows of the Soul* (Grand Rapids, Mich.: Zondervan, 1996), p. 217.

13. Many have benefited by placing these three phases within the timeline exercises suggested by Dr. J. Robert Clinton in *The Making of a Leader* (Colorado Springs, Colo.: NavPress, 1988) and in his other works.

14. Used with permission.

15. Philippians 1:6.

Acknowledgments

$\overline{=}\mathbf{W}$e are deeply grateful to those who in their wisdom loved us and who in their vulnerability were willing to earn our trust. For those who, in spite of what is true about us, continue to teach us about God's grace. And for those who introduced us to his dreams for our lives and now stand with us as we are privileged to share these truths with others.

Thanks to the board, staff, advisory council, and friends of Leadership Catalyst for your timeless encouragement and sacrificial investments. Special thanks go to Amanda Smith, Ellen Antill, and Mark Carver. Your "can do" spirit, skill, and friendship demonstrate why teamwork is better than solo work. We love that you are on our team!

We appreciate our dear friend, Stewart Black, a gifted theologian who expresses the message of this book through his life and teaching, and helped us clarify the biblical endnotes of *TrueFaced*.

Thanks to the men and women of Open Door Fellowship and The Neighborhood Church, with whom we are privileged to enjoy community and live in these truths.

Thanks to Alan Andrews and The Navigators National Leadership Team and many leaders, churches, and organizations who have proven the transferability of these truths during the past decade. The terrific NavPress team cared for this project with publishing expertise, energy, and encouragement. They include Kent Wilson, Dan Rich, Terry Behimer, Toben Heim, Greg Clouse, Don Simpson, Paul Santhouse,

Sarah Snelling, Monika Lewis, Candis Pflueger, Amy Slivka, Lisa Marshall, Kathleen Campbell, Jan Maniatis, and many other team members who are "difference makers." An immense debt of thanks goes to the outstanding editor NavPress secured for this project, Liz Heaney. Liz, you are a gift.

We are grateful for many volunteer readers and researchers who contributed their insights and significantly enriched this work. Deep thanks to our friends who live this message alongside us and who have given us permission to tell their stories. Finally, we would like to thank our families, who are the most loving and faithful mirrors of these truths in our lives, both when we are living in them and when we stray from them.

If you would like to know more about Leadership Catalyst, Inc. and its training programs and resources for leaders, families, organizations, institutions, and churches, please contact us at 888-249-0700 or visit our website at www.leadershipcatalyst.org.

Bill Thrall
Bruce McNicol
John Lynch

About Leadership Catalyst

──═**O**ne word has the power to catalyze greatness in an individual, an organization, or a nation: trust.

Surveys show that trust is the number one requirement for influence in life and leadership. But for many, trust has been hard to come by or misplaced. There is a painful Trust Gap . . . and it is widening in many arenas of the church, business, education, missions, government, and even family life.

The *mission* of Leadership Catalyst is *to build and restore trust in leaders and in those they influence.* Established in 1995, Leadership Catalyst is recognized as an international ministry of transformation for people who want to learn how to develop relationships of trust and environments of grace, which build character, authenticity, vision, and influence.

For the *individual,* Leadership Catalyst offers a variety of tools to help you build trust in your friendships, your family, and your community. Visit www.leadershipcatalyst.org for more details about Catalyst resources.

For the *organization,* Leadership Catalyst has designed a groundbreaking process to help leaders and teams bridge the Trust Gap. The High Trust Cultures™ process functions much like a computer operating system that accelerates all the programs in the computer. Delivery of the High Trust Cultures program is either self-guided or facilitated by Leadership Catalyst's team during an intensive multimonth residential and telecoaching program beginning with the

CEO and key members of their executive team and then moving into their organization. Visit www.leadershipcatalyst.org for details about the High Trust Cultures™ program.

LEADERSHIP
CATALYST

Leadership Catalyst, Inc.
E-mail: info@leadershipcatalyst.org
Website: www.leadershipcatalyst.org
Voice: 888-249-0700, toll-free in North America
Voice: 602-249-7000
Fax: 602-249-0611

Address:
1600 E. Northern Avenue, Suite 280
Phoenix, AZ 85020

About the Authors

BILL THRALL serves as leadership mentor for Leadership Catalyst, Inc. (LCI) and as a director on LCI's board. Prior to LCI, Bill led Open Door Fellowship in Phoenix, a church he established in 1973. Bill is also the coauthor of *The Ascent of a Leader* and *Beyond Your Best* (Jossey Bass), and continues to speak to people around the world about issues of trust, mentoring, and leadership. Bill lives in Phoenix with his wife, Grace. They have three children and seven grandchildren.

BRUCE MCNICOL guides Leadership Catalyst as president, combining international work experience and degrees in finance law, theology, and organizational development. He is a respected teacher and mentor for both established and emerging leaders in multiple cultures and contexts. Also the coauthor of *The Ascent of a Leader* and *Beyond Your Best* (Jossey Bass), Bruce is active as a speaker and mentor around the world. He lives in the Phoenix area with his wife, Janet, and their three children.

JOHN LYNCH is a national speaker for Leadership Catalyst, Inc. John is also the teaching pastor at Open Door Fellowship, and coleads Sharkey Productions, a drama outreach in Phoenix. He is a playwright and storyteller, and lives in Phoenix with his wife and three children.

"*TrueFaced* describes the kind of life I aspire to live."
—Dr. Joseph M. Stowell, president, Moody Bible Institute

A MESSAGE THAT WILL REVOLUTIONIZE YOUR SMALL GROUP AND SUNDAY SCHOOL CLASS.

An eight-week "experience guide" for small groups and individuals to explore the revolutionary concept of allowing ourselves the grace to be real with God and others.
TrueFaced Experience Guide
978-0-97709-089-1

In this eight-week DVD series, you and your small group will examine a revolutionary message of grace.
TrueFaced Experience DVD
(includes leader's guide)
978-0-97709-088-4

"One of the best books on practical theology I have seen."
—Dallas Willard, author of *Renovation of the Heart*

To order copies, Call Leadership Catalyst at 1-888-249-0700, or visit our website at www.leadershipcatalyst.org

▲ A Leadership *Catalyst* RESOURCE
www.leadershipcatalyst.org
1-888-249-0700